A PRACTICAL GUIDE FOR
DEVELOPING MEDIUMSHIP

THE
EVIDENTIAL
MEDIUM

Kay Reynolds

To Mom, for teaching me about
God's messengers on Earth.
And to Dad, for his gentle nudge from the spirit world,
encouraging me to embrace my mediumistic gifts.

Before you can touch the Spirit, you must find it within yourself, for all truth, all knowledge and all loving must first be found within oneself.

—Gordon Higginson

FOREWORD

by Jason Goldsworthy

I've been aware of the spirit world my entire life but suppressed my experiences until the passing of my brother. At that time, I could no longer deny this ability I held within. I was working in a hospital at the time and was around death daily. It's funny how life takes us down pathways that lead us to our destiny. Realizing I could no longer ignore my truths, I began to pay attention to the phenomena occurring around me, which sparked my interest further. I went on to study intently with some of the finest mediums of our times at the renowned Arthur Findlay College. I now hold CSNU certificates in speaking and demonstrating and am currently working toward my certificate in teaching.

I was introduced to Kay Reynolds through my training. We were both mentored by Mavis Pittilla and trained with many of the same tutors at the Arthur Findlay College. As the years passed by, a friendship developed and our journey as mediums began. We traveled throughout England and Europe working in churches and theaters. Since Kay's return to the United States, we have continued our collaboration, doing workshops and lectures online.

It's been interesting to watch Kay grow and blossom into the medium she is today. When I first met Kay, she was at the beginning of her journey; she was shy and unsure of herself. You wouldn't know that now, watching her work or listening to her speak. I watched her take in every bit of knowledge from our tutors. She was like a sponge during her training years. She nourished her spiritual growth carefully, taking the time to go within and learn about her own true essence.

I found it fascinating to watch Kay dissect mediumship in her training. She turned mediumship upside down, took it apart and looked at it from every angle, so she could understand the meaning of what it is to be a medium. It wasn't enough for her to make a contact, it wasn't enough to know how to deliver the mechanics of mediumship. She had to know what made a medium tick, how the spirit world interacted with her – and her with them.

Kay has a lovely way of synthesizing the knowledge she learned from all her tutors and presenting it in a way that makes sense to her, and ultimately, to her students. She breaks it down into small, bite-sized pieces of information so as to not overwhelm the students. She understands the importance of the work mediums do and is dedicated to guiding those who are on this path.

It's important for those interested in mediumship to be knowledgeable about all things mediumistic. Mediums need to move beyond the mechanics and understand the how's and why's of mediumship too. In *The Evidential Medium*, Kay has given readers a step-by-step approach to help them delve into a deeper understanding of mediumship and all it encompasses (from Kay's perspective), while at the same time bringing her funny, caring personality to the forefront. By reading this book, mediums will be able to relate to Kay's stories, and through doing the exercises they'll be able to experience the mediumship journey for themselves.

Training to be a medium can be confusing. There are many different opinions about mediumship and it all entails, much of which is not true—or misleading at best. It's important to find teachers who are down-to-earth, and who will bring knowledge forward in an understandable way. The thing about mediumship is you really must go through development, and you must practice and learn. All three of these things are necessary to grow as a medium and students need a knowledgeable guide to help them along the way. Learning about all aspects of mediumship removes the guesswork and takes you into the full potential of your ability.

At some point, we must ask ourselves, "Am I okay with being mediocre or do I want to rise to my full potential?" The more work you put into your development, the greater the reward for you the medium, your recipient, and the spirit communicator. If you are serious about your development as a medium, this book will help you understand the true expressions of your soul, move beyond your comfort zone, and polish your mediumship. It will guide you and help you to reach your fullest potential. Learning to be a medium doesn't happen overnight. To begin to see your potential, you must put in the effort—jut as I did, and just as Kay did. The journey to becoming a medium is important and you are very much needed in the world. I wish you all a happy and productive journey.

Jason Goldsworthy, CSNU
www.jasongoldsworthy.com

ACKNOWLEDGMENTS

I would like to thank my mentor, Mavis Pittilla, for her loving support, patience, and knowledge. Without you, I don't know if I would have made it.

Jean Else, where do I begin to express how much you have impacted my presence on stage? I will forever hear your encouraging words in my ear. Thank you!

Paul Jacobs, you are an infinite vessel of wisdom. Thank you for your generous sharing of knowledge and time.

Thanks to everyone on the PRESStinely team. Special thanks to Kristen, for answering my million and one questions and keeping me on track, Maira for leading the way in social media (you are a genius), and Dawn for your amazing design talents.

A huge thank you to Michael Ireland for being an editor extraordinaire. You are a Goddess!

Finally, thank you to my students and readers for your support and your dedication to the wonderful craft of mediumship. May you continue to develop your gifts and to serve the spirit world in the highest possible way. I wish you every success on your journey. You've got this!

Love, Kay

LIST OF ILLUSTRATIONS AND IMAGES

TABLES LIST

TABLE OF CONTENTS

CHAPTER 1

"SOUL RISING"

I didn't set out to be a medium. I'm a teacher. That's what I do. I'm a mom. I'm a grandmother. I'm a daughter. I'm a sister. That's me. Being a medium didn't exactly fit into my plan. Yet, here I am.

If I go all the way back into my earliest memories of being a child, I can remember seeing the spirit world. I remember it clearly. What stands out is the incredible feeling of love I felt in that moment—that split-second moment left a lasting impression on me. That's for sure.

I didn't see the spirit people much but I always knew they were there. Not one. Not two. Not even three. There was a sea of them for as far as I could see, as far as I could feel. I called them my angels. I don't know why. Perhaps because of my Christian upbringing. When I was five, my family moved to Japan and I remember as I sat on my bunk bed playing with my Barbie dolls, I saw a Native Indian ... he was definitely not an angel. He stayed with me and I now know him as one of my guides. But, more importantly, he is my partner on my spiritual journey.

I spent the first half of my life not understanding the phenomena happening around me. I became an expert at either ignoring it or not giving it much thought. Once I asked my mom why people I didn't know came to me in my dreams with messages for her. She explained that God needed people on Earth to deliver messages from Heaven, that He had chosen me, and that I should feel honored to be God's messenger. As a child, that was all the explanation I needed.

As a young adult, however, my curiosity increased, but I didn't know where to turn. I learned to "zip my lip" when it came to seeing the dead. Most people thought I was nuts. So, I wandered around aimlessly, not understanding what was happening to me. With each new experience, a thousand more questions came.

Fast forward to adulthood. After being married and having children, I became a reading teacher. I was quite content teaching children in a small town in Texas. As life goes, I got a divorce and raised my children. I went on to get a master's in education and my school principal certification but something was still missing. My youngest child was out of high school and had joined the army. Living alone gave me time to reflect on what I wanted to do with the next chapter of my life. Growing up as a child of the military, I had a love for travel and I knew there were military schools overseas. I thought, "What a perfect job!" I applied and within a few months had an offer to move to Germany and be a reading specialist on an army post.

I had been living in Germany for six years when I was diagnosed with a rare lung disease. My doctor and I searched all over Europe trying to find a physician who could treat me and I ended up having to travel to America for surgery. Eventually, I found a doctor in London who researched my disease and took me on. A year later, I received a medical transfer from Germany to England. Funny thing, I knew I wasn't moving to England because of my health. There was a much bigger reason.

I settled into my new home in Fordham, in a 300-year-old barn conversion. Every time I walked into the kitchen, I heard a cow moo—even though there were no cows nearby. Living in houses with paranormal activity was not new to me, but that was my first spirit cow! I was at home in that house; it still makes me laugh when I think about it.

Everything about my life had changed—and there was a change in me too. More and more, I noticed the spirit world. As my curiosity grew, I conducted experiments in communicating with my Dad, who had passed twenty-three years before. I made ridiculous commands, seeking proof that I was really communicating with him. My dad obliged—in fact, he blew me away. Then one day, out of the blue, I had a visit from two spirit people: the father and wife of a friend of mine, Ross. They gave me their names and information about themselves and asked me to say hello to Ross for them. Later, I gave Ross the information—and he confirmed it all.

This got my attention! I was no longer talking to just Dad, I was talking to complete strangers. Hoping to prove the theory of me-as-nutcase wrong, I turned to my trusted friend Google, to see if there was anywhere I could go to learn more about spirit world phenomena. I discovered the wonderful Arthur Findlay College in Stansted, England, where mediums from around the world trained. I lived within an hour of Arthur Findlay College! I looked at the list of courses and thought, "There's no way I can go there. What do I know about mediumship?" It took a couple of years, but I finally summoned the courage to go.

I will never forget the first time I walked into the Great Hall just beyond the reception desk. I was home! Many mediums have felt the same way—I knew right then I'd be coming back again and again.

Through the years, while I maintained a busy teaching schedule on a US military base, I attended week-long intensives at Arthur Findlay College several times a year. I was fortunate, finding tutors who had studied under the late, great Gordon Higginson. I decided early in my development that all of my tutors had to have been trained by him. Everyone I met told me, "You must take a course with Mavis Pittilla." I knew nothing about this "Mavis chick," but I knew there must be something very special about her, and there was: Mavis was Gordon Higginson's first mentorship student.

I had just completed a course with a gentleman in Wales, one of Mavis' former students. He had organized a course in Eastbourne and I signed up. To my surprise, he put me with Mavis. On the first morning, Mavis walked into our classroom and wowed me instantly. As she spoke, I held onto every word—it was as if she was speaking directly to me and there was no one else in the room. My eyes watered, my throat tightened. Within minutes, she touched my soul in a way no other tutor had ever done. I had found my mentor. I went on to take three fifteen-month mentorship programs with Mavis. There is no way to measure all I learned from her. I will be forever grateful for her generosity in sharing her knowledge and skill.

As well as studying with Mavis, I took classes at Arthur Findlay College. All the tutors at the College were either trained by Gordon Higginson or were trained by one of Gordon's students. They were the best of the best.

Most of my classes were with the last student Gordon mentored, Paul Jacobs. Looking back, I know that this is why the door to England opened for me—I was sent there to learn from the top mediums in the world.

My training with Mavis and the tutors at Arthur Findlay College was intense. There were days when I cried, days when I cursed, and days when I wanted to give it all up. But I couldn't quit. A little voice in my head kept whispering: "Keep going." So, I did.

I am thankful for the wisdom my tutors shared and for how they all helped to shape my mediumship development. They saw something in me I couldn't see. They were both tough and gentle when I needed it—they pushed me beyond my comfort zone.

For many years, I studied under great mediums. As I sat in the library or the lecture room at Arthur Findlay College, immersed in the history of the pioneers of mediumship, I thought back to when I was trying to make sense of my spirit world experience. I wondered, "Where was this training when I was young?"

I knew I wanted to help mediums who found themselves in the same place I'd been in all those years ago. I wanted to reach out to mediums who lived in remote areas and had nowhere to go to get answers. I knew the British style of evidential mediumship was a new concept in America, and thoughts of teaching in the United States meandered through my mind. Ideas for books rose to the surface. Of course, with today's technology, I can reach mediums far beyond the borders of America—which makes it even sweeter!

After eleven years of living in England and teaching children, I turned in my early retirement paperwork to say goodbye to the classroom and the children I loved dearly. Within two weeks, my house was packed and my cat and I were flying home to the US. I knew the road ahead would not be easy, that there would be endless work. I didn't care. I embraced it all with my whole heart. I couldn't wait to bring to fruition all the thoughts that had wandered through my head while I'd been learning about the unseen world.

After brainstorming for book ideas, *The Evidential Medium: A Practical Guide for Developing Mediumship* was born. I wrote this book for mediums who can already make contact with the spirit world and for those who are ready to begin working on their own but want to stretch and take their mediumship to the next level.

I've written this book to share with you the practical exercises I did in my training with my tutors and to move you beyond your comfort zone. Each chapter covers specific mediumship skills with examples and exercises. You'll hear stories of my training: the good, the bad, and the "Oh crap" moments. I lay it all out for you, as I believe it's important to know that the struggles are real. Everything you are going through ... I'm pretty sure I've gone through it too.

As a reading specialist in public schools for twenty-nine years, I followed the KISS method: *Keep It Simple, Silly.* I believe that teaching mediumship should follow the same format. There is no need to complicate things. Mediumship is tough enough, let's keep it simple.

The exercises here are for you to do over and over again. You can't become a medium overnight. I trained hard for seven years before becoming a professional medium; I sat with my guide for a year before beginning my training. Yep, that's true! So, if you decide to hang with me and go through this book, hunker down. Get ready to work hard and practice, practice, practice.

But remember: the thoughts and ideas I present in this book are my own opinion and represent my truths. As you train and learn from various tutors as I did, you will form your own truths.

Remember too that neither I nor any other medium can turn you into a medium. Your mediumship tools have been within you all along. The only thing teachers of mediumship can do is help you to awaken those gifts, show you ways to tweak what you are already doing to enhance your mediumship, and help you let go of bad habits.

My hope is that you will take something from this book that resonates deep within your soul and inspires you to grab hold of your truths and walk your path proudly. Take my successes and my failures and use them to navigate your own unique journey. Throw out what doesn't resonate. Hold on to what touches your soul.

As noted, do the exercises over and over: Each time you revisit them, you will learn something new. Get to know your guide as I know mine. There is no greater teacher than those in the unseen world who signed up to walk this journey with you.

Lastly, embrace the spiritual gifts that are buried in your soul. You have everything you need to walk your path of truth. The only thing holding you back is you. Your life plan is already set. So, get on with it.

Your soul is ready to rise.

How to Read this Book

I believe in "going with the flow." As I was writing this book, the teacher in me wanted to bust out and use tried-and-true teaching techniques. It may seem a little geeky but I went with it and allowed "Ms. Reynolds" to shine through. It's just me being me—hopefully, it will help you. I think it's safe to say that "You can take the teacher out of the classroom but you'll never take the classroom out of the teacher."

So, in keeping with a "teaching modality," at the end of each chapter, you'll find some type of exercise or meditation to do, and (from time to time) there will be handouts to guide you in the exercise. I've given you step-by-step instructions, a list of supplies you'll need, and suggestions on how many people are needed for each exercise. The exercises are to be followed by discussion with your sitter. You can do the soul journey reflection and journaling on your own. I wasn't joking: If you hang with me and this book, there is work ahead! To make this work for you:

1. As you move through *The Evidential Medium*, I recommend you find a small group of mediums or sitters to work with. It is best if they are reading this book too. In a way, you'll be forming a "Mediums" book club. You can work in person—or, if you don't know any mediums near you, online via Zoom, Skype, or Facebook Messenger is a great alternative. Please join my Facebook group, "Medium's Corner," where you will find other mediums who will be happy to work with you. If you can't find a full group for your book club, then practice with any willing person in your social circle.
2. Go to my website. There you will find free journal pages and a Medium's Club Membership you can join. The

Medium's Club provides tutorial videos and handouts of the exercises in the book.

3. You will need a journal for reflection and soul journeying. You can purchase a journal or create a journal notebook using the journal pages on my website. (My website URL and others are listed at the end of this book.) Whatever you decide, you may want to consider creating a place to assemble the handouts. You'll use these handouts throughout your mediumship journey. The handouts are part of the Medium's Club Membership. You can also create your own using the examples in this book as a template.

4. Once you form your book club, before you meet with them, go to my website and download the journal pages if needed.

5. At your first group meeting, decide on the number of chapters you want to read by a specific date. See the example BELOW.

Table #1: Chapters Read/Meeting Dates

Chapters Read	Meeting Dates
Chapters 1-2	August 1
Chapters 3	August 15
Chapters 4	September 1
Chapters 5	September 15

6. At your first group practice session, review the instructions and expectations for the medium and the sitters. Do the exercises. After practice, discuss the checklists, if any, to see how the medium did. Use the discussion questions at the end of each chapter and reflect on them. Allow your thoughts to flow and bring you new, meaningful revelations.

7. Later, find some quiet time, grab your journal and a pen, and write your soul a letter. Allow your soul to respond through automatic writing.
8. Please check my website for new courses, classes and free resources.
9. I also have a YouTube channel with video tutorials. Head on over there, hit the subscribe button, and have a watch party.

The Evidential Medium: A Practical Guide for Developing Mediumship is designed so that you can revisit its pages throughout your mediumship development. Remember, mediumship development does not happen overnight—you'll need to do these exercises many times. I did them over a seven-year period and still revisit them. Over time, they became easier and my understanding of each exercise became clearer. Some will be easy from the start, some will need a lot of extra practice. That's normal. Think of doing these exercises as planting seeds of knowledge. Each time you revisit an exercise, you nurture those seeds. One day, the seeds you planted will stand strong and tall and will bear fruit.

She believed she could, so she did.

—R.S. Grey

Chapter 2

"Naked to the Bone"

When I heard it, I was standing in a mediumship class, in front of my peers, bringing everything I had. My heart was pounding, I was shaking. Earlier, I had watched as one by one, all the other mediums stood up to give their demonstrations. No one had to force them. They stood with confidence as if they had done this many times before—and they had. They were all so polished! There were no long pauses, no "Ummm's," "I think's," or "I'm not sure's." One piece of evidence after another rolled off their lips. I was in awe. I could have sat there all day, watching them work.

I'd sat in my seat praying that when it was my turn, someone from the spirit world would come. The longer I sat, the worse my nerves got. "Why am I even here?" I didn't want to get up in front of everyone and try to make a contact with the spirit world. "Who am I," I thought, "in this room full of amazing mediums, to even think I'm a medium?"

We were to meet every other month south of London at a spiritual center called the Banyan Retreat. The Banyan was small but very nice with a wonderful energy and situated on beautiful grounds. On this first day of mentorship, there was a small group of experienced mediums sitting in the back two rows of the room. All of them had worked as mediums for ten, fifteen, twenty years. It wasn't that I was afraid to stand and speak in front of an audience, I had done that many times. As a teacher in Texas, I'd often spoken at teacher's conventions, school board meetings, and principals' conferences. I'd also taught teachers. Standing in front of people wasn't the problem.

The problem with standing at the front of a room preparing to do mediumship is that there is no preparing what you are going to say. As a keynote speaker, I'd had an outline, a PowerPoint. I knew exactly what I was going to present. It's not that way as a medium—you stand up there, exposed. No script, no outline. Buck Naked. You don't know what's going to happen, who (if anyone) will show up, if anyone in your audience will be able to take the information. You're at the mercy of the spirit world and your own inner power. So, you bring all you have to offer.

Then you hope and pray it's enough to make the contact.

Silently, I asked my guide to come. I couldn't feel him. "Where are you?" My hands were clammy, my stomach was clenching into a knot. I was a beginner, what did I have to offer? In my opinion, not much. I was not like the other mediums in the room. I sat there, scared out of my wits. When I made my way to the front of the room, what would happen?

All twenty-three of the other mediums in the room had given a reading. I was the last one. I stood up, walked past the group in the back. One of them gasped. "Why did she gasp? Was she gasping at me? If yes, why?" I wanted to run: out the door, down the hall, out to my car, never come back. The knot in my stomach was twisting. "I can't do this."

All eyes were on me. I walked to the front. I lowered my head, said one more prayer. I looked up, looked out at everyone waiting eagerly for me to do my thing. I looked over at my tutor. She gave me the nod to begin.

I lowered my head again and closed my eyes. I don't know why. Maybe to shut everyone out. Maybe to focus. Maybe to pray. I cried out silently for my guide to come—for anyone to come. After what seemed like forever, I opened my eyes, lifted my head. The mediums in the back rows were whispering to each other.

I began to speak. "I feel that I have a grandmother." After a long pause, I gave another piece of evidence, then another. Whose grandmother did I have? I had no idea. I wasn't like those experienced mediums—they knew exactly who they had and who the recipient was. I was thankful to have someone, anyone, thankful that I was getting a piece of evidence, thankful that whatever was churning in my stomach was staying down.

My eyes kept taking me to an area at the back of the room—not to the side where the whispering was coming from, thank God. I gave a few more bits of evidence and asked if anyone understood it. A woman sitting right where my eyes kept taking me raised her hand. I took a deep breath and continued. Another "Yes" from her. My nerves were settling a bit. I could still hear the nervous rattle in my voice but I was calming down enough that I could connect a little stronger with this grandmother.

Then the most amazing thing happened. This grandmother took me on a journey. Images flashed through my mind; flickering like old television movies as the film is rolling. This flickering movie was playing in my mind ... moving quickly across a beautiful piece of land ... huge rolling hills ... vibrant green. Nothing like you see back home in Texas. I could see the ocean in the distance. All of a sudden, I felt as if I was in Ireland.

I described what I was seeing, what I felt, the smell of the ocean as we got closer to it. The woman in the audience said "Yes, I understand." I continued, describing a house in the distance ... a tall, narrow house, light in color ... three, maybe more floors. The woman said "Yes." The grandmother opened the front door, we went inside. I described the entryway ... stairs to the right just in front ... a long narrow hallway ... a door to the left .... it led into a small sitting area ... in the back of the house, a kitchen ... a door that went to the back garden. "Yes," the woman said, "I know exactly where you are."

The grandmother took me upstairs. It felt as if we were flying up the stairs to the next floor, as if she couldn't get there fast enough. Up one floor, then to the next, all the way to the top. She took me into a room: a bed ... a tiny window ... a rocking chair ... a throw rug on the floor. This was her room, where she spent most of her days toward the end of her life, too frail to come downstairs. She shared with me her memories of children coming to see her in this room. She had a box that she kept toys in for the little ones. She often stared out the window, dreaming of her younger days, her husband who had long ago passed. She loved this house. She loved this land. Most of all, she loved her family. The woman in the audience said "Yes" to all the evidence.

She said "Yes!" Did you read that line? She said "Yes!" What? Really? "Yes?" All my nerves, the sick feeling in the pit of my stomach faded away. I'd done it! I'd survived. I'd made contact with the spirit world. "Thank you, Jesus," I thought.

I turned to my tutor to receive her critique. The nerves didn't take long to get going again. There I stood, in front of everyone, feeling naked, waiting. "Oh God, what did she think?" She must have known how scared I was, that it was all I could do to keep my lunch in my belly.

My tutor was kind, gentle. She said she particularly liked the way I allowed the grandmother to take me on a "mind journey." I'd never heard of a mind journey before that day. I wondered exactly what it was, how it had happened. Her only critique was to not allow myself to linger too long in one place when I go on mind journeys. She didn't mind the long pauses between my bits of evidence. She didn't mind my nerves. She found my strength in the reading, told me what was good about it, what I could do to make it better. That's what good teachers do, you know. They find your strength, point it out, and lead you to the next step.

I didn't understand the "mind journey," I said. "Did I do that, or was it spirit?"

That's when I heard it. It went right up my spine: The mediums at the back snickered. My heart sank. Self-doubt crashed in, consumed me, took control. "Why had they laughed? What had I done wrong?" I wanted to bolt, out the door, down the hall, into my car. "Didn't they know how hard it was for me to stand in front of them? Had they forgotten that they too were once exactly where I was?" I made my way back to my chair, passing right in front of them. It was humiliating, having to sit in front of them. I was mortified. So, I sat down and burrowed deep into a safe space I built around me. I assembled an imaginary concrete bunker that the echoes of their laughter couldn't get through.

That night, back in my hotel room, I cried. I doubted my ability as a medium. I wanted to go home. But the next morning, I went back and faced those mediums. I did! I could have been mad at them for laughing. Instead, I befriended them. I got to know them. I even became grateful for them. You see, that was my first lesson in being tough as a medium. If I wanted to make it as a medium I had to be tough. My stubbornness came to the forefront. Stubbornness comes in handy when you crash and burn. And, let me tell you, there was a lot of crashing and burning.

My mom always said, "If you want to be great, you have to hang around those you think are greater than you. Being the best at your game," she said, "means you must learn from the best." I held tight to her words—they were my lifeline.

I may not have been the best in that class. I may even have been the worst. That's okay. I was hanging out with mediums who had walked this path and I believed they were far greater than me. I could learn from them.

So, weekend after weekend, I stood before those mediums whom I called the "greats" and bared my soul to work with the spirit world. Like I said, I may as well have been stark naked standing in front of them—it was that hard. But I did it. I brought everything I had, used all that I had. I may have been scruffy, muddy, and I may have been a hot mess half the time. That's okay. I did it. We all have to start somewhere. I took the criticism, learned how to turn it around. I celebrated every tiny milestone. I clung to mom's words—my fighting words. That's what it takes sometimes.

A few years later, I was chatting with one of those great mediums who had snickered at me.

He brought up that moment. "Why the hell is he bringing this up?" I stood there, frozen. He shared that they had all felt the power of my energy when I stood up and walked past them. They had all gasped silently (except for the one who had let that audible gasp slip from her lips) and they'd stared at one another in disbelief. Then they'd whispered together—they were worried about having to work with me! They laughed because I was so naive about the power I had within me. They couldn't believe I didn't know.

Me? My power? Little ole' me, just starting this journey? They worried about me? I stood there in disbelief, fighting back tears. The greats had seen (or felt) something in me I didn't know I had. They weren't laughing because I was a bad medium, they didn't gasp because they didn't think I could do it. They felt a greatness within me, a greatness I'd been oblivious to at the time. But my ego, my self-doubt, and my lack of confidence took that gasp and their whispers and made them negative. That's what we human beings do. I'd allowed my own negative thoughts to control me for a long time. My battle wasn't with the greats. My battle was with me.

That's all part of the journey, facing your fears, healing the doubts within you, discovering your true essence, and—as hard as it may seem—moving forward. We have to learn to believe in ourselves.

I'm grateful for the greats. They may never know how they affected my life but they did—in so many wonderful ways. I know there are many mediums who are just starting out on this journey who are experiencing these same fears and self-doubts, and who are wondering, "Who am I to think I'm a medium?" I'll tell you who you are. You're the next "great." You came into this world as a medium. You have a power within you that you haven't met yet but it's right there, waiting for you to unlock the chains that bind it, waiting for you: *the next great medium*.

Go on. Find your courage. Stand there, bare your soul, be naked to the bone. Allow your soul to rise.

This is Your Journey

I learned several lessons that day (and throughout the next fifteen months of my first mentorship). The first lesson was: *This is my journey, I must not compare it to anyone else's. I alone hold the key to turn my journey into something great.* Instead of waiting to go last on the speaker platform, I learned it was better to go early, so my nerves didn't get the best of me.

Reaching out to the greats was a huge plus. Becoming friends with them gave me the opportunity to watch them—and even work with them later. They took me under their wings. Instead of being the snickering voices inside my head, they became a vital, encouraging part of my journey.

I learned several other lessons in my first mentorship too. Among them were learning to trust myself and the spirit world, and learning to take a leap of faith every time I did a reading.

Trust

That first mentorship was the beginning of my journey to Trust. Trust is the hardest lesson of all. It didn't happen overnight—in fact, it took two more mentorships before I could say confidently that I trusted in myself and the spirit world.

I know what you're thinking: "I trust myself. I trust the spirit world completely." Yep, I said that too. I said it over and over. I thought I trusted—but there was one simple problem. I hadn't taken those words in. They were just words, sputtering across my lips. On the inside, I wasn't convinced, I still had fears, still had healing to do. Over the years, as I healed and let go of my fears, I began to trust from the inside out. That's what we all have to do.

Take that Leap of Faith

I was a hot mess that first day. Truthfully, I was a mess on the last day too—but hopefully a lukewarm one. I was finding my way. I was confident enough to know that taking the leap of faith to give mediumship a try was exactly what my soul had needed. Slowly, I began to trust the evidence as it came in and would just give what I got. I was pleasantly surprised to discover that most of what I gave as evidence was correct. I even became more accepting of the No's. I learned that No's are my best friends. I learned the most from No's.

It doesn't matter where you are on your journey, your insecurities will always come bubbling up to hinder you. So, change your thought process. Every time you connect to the Divine, instead of seeing your failures or thinking that your evidence is weak, see the miracle. Celebrate the miracles. We have to rise above our own fears, insecurities, and lack of confidence. This is the journey of our soul. Our soul knows exactly why it is here on Earth. It has all the tools it needs to do the work it came to do. When we surrender to our destiny, we find that the road gets a little easier.

So, my friends, surrender, let go ... and fly.

Journaling

Your journal is a place you can write down your reflections and private thoughts. You will also use your journal to write letters to your soul or to the spirit within you—these two parts of you work so closely together, they are almost interchangeable. It makes no difference if you choose to write "to your soul" or "to your spirit."

Before I found my mentor, I was using meditation to go within, to learn about me, and to bring inner healing to the battle wounds of life. An unexpected added bonus was getting to know my guide. In the process, I wrote letters to my guide, hoping he would communicate with me.

One day, I discovered that it wasn't my guide responding. I knew without question that it was my soul giving me encouragement. That was the beginning—I was getting to know me. I wrote about what was puzzling me, about my fears, frustrations, and happy moments. I always ended with a question, asking, "What wisdom did you want me to know?" Holding the pen in my hand, I closed my eyes and became still within. I'd wait for a nudge, then start writing. At first, the writings were short and didn't always make sense. With time, however, they became long, beautiful messages. I still go back from time to time and read some of those letters. I'm always amazed at how profound the messages of love and hope were.

It is my wish for you to develop a relationship with your soul too. Here's a sample of my letters to my soul, and my soul's reply.

Dear Soul,

It seems as if my days run together. I often wonder if I am losing my mind. Am I really a medium? Can I really speak to those who have died? I want to believe it, I really do. When I do make a connection, I feel like I am on top of the world. In those moments, I know I am on the right track. Then there are the times when I struggle with making a contact and I doubt that I am a medium. I try and try and try but feel as if I am going nowhere. Thank you for listening to me. Do you have any words of wisdom for me today? Love, K

Dearest Child,

I know at times it seems as if you are moving nowhere, as if you are hitting one wall after another. It is not so, my child. It is the natural progression of your soul's journey, learning how to navigate through the winding path to unlock the wisdom you hold within.

If only you could see yourself in the way I see you or the view your helpers see from the unseen world. For you see, we see only illumination of beauty from your being. We see the subtle changes of which you are unaware. Your light shines brighter with each passing moment. You touch those around you, oblivious to how your light penetrates through and touches their soul.

You are exactly where we need you on your journey. You are perfect in every way. You are a spark of the Divine. You are love and you are loved beyond measure. Go within to seek knowledge and understanding. It is there, you'll find all you need.

Celebrate each step you take. Celebrate the no's. Celebrate the yes's. Celebrate the tears and celebrate the joy. You are on a sacred path and all that you do has the thread of Divinity shining through.

This is my prayer for you,

Eternal love.

Getting Organized

As noted earlier, I recommend that you create a special place to keep all of your reflections and soul letters, as well as your notes, checklists, and exercises from this book. Having everything in one place will provide an easily accessible reference for you in the future. There are several ways to do this:

1. Create a journal or notebook with tabs or pocket dividers separating the chapters.
2. Download the journal sheets from my website at *www.kayreynolds.org*. You can join the Medium's Club (Members-Only) group to download all of the exercise handouts.
3. Assemble your pages together by chapter.
4. The second choice would be to buy a pre-made notebook, preferably one with pocket dividers, to add your exercise sheets and checklists.

EXERCISE 1

The Spirit Within Meditation and Soul Letter

Objective 1:

The aim of the meditation is to help you meet your spirit within so you may begin to understand the true expressions of you.

Objective 2:

The aim of writing a letter to your soul is to develop a relationship or partnership with your soul.

Materials Needed:

- Journal.
- Guided Meditation.
- Self.

Table #2: Expectations: The Spirit Within Meditation

Expectations The Spirit Within Meditation	
Medium's Role	**Recipient's Role**
• Meditate to meet the soul • Write a letter to your soul • Use automatic writing to allow your soul to respond	• Not Applicable

Procedures:

1. Below is a condensed version of the meditation. You may you use these words to create your own meditation, or go to my website (*www.kayreynolds.org*) to listen to the version I recorded.
2. After the meditation, connect with your soul.

MEDITATION

The Spirit Within Introduction

Spiritual development is the core component of developing as a medium. It is the building of a relationship with your creator, the God source. It is the falling away of the material aspects of your life, uncovering the depths of your being so the true expression of your soul may rise. It is living in oneness with your Creator.

The epigraph I used (by Gordon Higginson, one of the greatest mediums of the twentieth century) is powerful on its own. I thought it only fitting to include the rest of what Gordon said during his lecture at the Arthur Findlay College:

> *Before you can touch the Spirit, you must find it within yourself, for all truth, all knowledge and all loving must first be found within oneself. The Spirit can never touch you and bring love and peace within your being and from your being until you have it for yourself. And, before you can build a picture of love from Spirit, you must learn to find it in this life. Always prepare yourself as a channel for Spirit, stand there with love radiating from you, and then God will touch you. (paraphrased)*

Let us begin.

Close your eyes. Take a few deep breaths to clear your mind and then return your breathing to a normal rhythm.

Relax

With each breath in and each breath out, relax, letting go of tensions in the body, letting go of thoughts.

> *I believe we are spiritual beings living here in a physical body, having a human experience. Our spirit within the confines of our body comes from the unseen world.*

> *I want to invite you to come along with me on a journey. A journey to get to know the spirit within.*

Breathe in a comfortable rhythm. Relax. Focus on your breath. Breathing still, fall into the silence of you.

Breathe.

Moving your focus to the center of your being, notice a bright light. A light of pure white shining from within.

Focus on the light.

See it growing and becoming brighter.

Imagine it moving through your body, filling every cell of your being.

This light emanates from the core of your being. It is who you truly are, a spirit being, a light being.

With each breath in and each breath out, the light within becomes more intense and moves beyond the confines of your body.

It moves outward, surrounding your physical body, expanding still, until it fills the whole room.

Stay here in this spot just for a moment, allowing this light to wrap you in love. Breathe it in. Experience it.

This is you, your true essence, the spirit within.

You are a Divine being, the spirit within, made of pure light, perfect in every way.

Relaxing, still breathing, imagine if in you will that in just a moment, you will stand up but leave your physical body in the chair.

Breathe. Become more still, more relaxed.

Imagine your spirit body standing up, leaving the physical body behind. See your spirit body standing there just in front of you.

Know you are loved, you are safe, held in the hands of your Creator.

Take in the feeling of your spirit within. It is free at this moment, standing before you. Breathe.

See the light shining from your spiritual body.

Imagine now, the light of your Creator moving toward you, surrounding you and ready to join your light.

Breathe.

Enjoy this beautiful connection, how you feel, and any sensations. Take it all in, breathe.

You are touching the energy of all knowing, all loving, and all truth. Our time is drawing to a close.

See yourself sitting there in the room. Your spirit body is joining your physical body, they become one again.

Your spirit body plays an important role in your mediumship.

When you work with the spirit world, it is through your spirit body that they try to connect. All communication is through your spirit body.

As you move forward on your spiritual journey of learning to be a medium, become more aware of the role that your spirit body—also known as your etheric body—has in your development.

Communication is from spirit to spirit.

You can connect with the spirit within at any time.

Call upon your spirit for inspiration, for wisdom, and for direction. You hold the key to all truths, all knowing, and all loving.

Search within.

Namaste

Soul Letter

- Think of a question you want guidance about, either in your personal life or on your mediumship journey. Write your question down in your journal—be concise.

- Close your eyes. Take a few deep breaths. Relax. You can do this by meditating, breathing deeply, and visualizing yourself being calm and still.
- Enter into a light trance state. You can enter into a light trance by listening to music, saying a mantra, doing self-hypnosis, or using a guided meditation. A light trance is similar to a child zoning out with a video game or while watching TV.
- When you are ready, begin writing. Write whatever comes to you. Do not worry about whether it is you or your soul writing. Just write. Allow the information to flow.
- It is common for your mind to interfere at first. If this happens, return to the light trance state. Eventually, your soul will take over and your mind will step back. It may take weeks or even months of practice. That's okay. Set your intention. Keep going.

The truest expression of soul is when Spirit illuminates your being in all you do.

—Kay Reynolds

Chapter 3

"The Soul's Expression"

Since you chose to read this book, it's likely you've been developing your psychic and mediumistic abilities for a while. You have a pretty good grasp of what is going on but maybe you are seeking an extra boost or a bit more understanding in certain areas. My hope is that the brief information in this chapter will give you ideas to ponder and guidance on how best to move forward with the exercises in this book.

The Soul's Expression

Almost all wobbles in our mediumship are a reflection of our personal soul development. If only I had a nickel for every time a tutor told me, "Kay, you need to work on yourself some more" ... and I walked away sighing, rolling my eyes, and mumbling under my breath. Yes, it's true, from time to time, I did do that. Okay—maybe I did it a lot. But in the end, I'd take the advice and go work on myself.

Whether we realize it or not, we work on ourselves when we sit quietly in meditation with our soul. When we sit in the power of the God source, we discover answers to questions like, "What is the true essence of my soul?" and "What is my purpose in life?" When we discover these things, we can allow our soul to guide us in expressing those qualities in this life.

We all choose our paths in life—many times over. The trick is learning how to let your soul make the choice. At one time, for example, I wanted to be a school principal. I had just finished a master's degree in education and spent a lot of money and time going directly into a second master's. But once I finished it, I no longer wanted to be a principal—I never used that second degree. What happened? Instead of letting my soul express its true desire, I'd let my mind choose.

The key is finding the true expressions of our soul, then letting them shine forth and light our paths. Of course, we all have more than one soul path. For me, my first path was teaching; my soul is not complete without being a teacher. Everywhere I go, in all that I do, I find teachable moments. The second pathway of my soul is creativity: using color and being surrounded by beauty in all things makes me feel alive. Finally, mediumship is my third path, an expression of my soul that fills me up beyond measure.

As I told you earlier, I've been aware of the spirit world my whole life. While my curiosity and my desire to learn more about it was sparked in my twenties, the feeling that "This is my life's path" didn't come until my late forties. At that point, the feeling was so strong that I developed tunnel vision—I dedicated my life to learning about mediumship.

The first stage of becoming a medium is taking a spiritual journey within, understanding yourself, touching the spiritual quality of your soul, and finding peace. You know your spiritual awakening has begun when the desire to choose a path in life becomes so strong you can't say no. When we find that true expression of our soul and allow it to awaken and express itself, our lives become meaningful, even powerful. We find the inner strength to overcome obstacles and fulfill our soul's purpose. Next, we connect with a higher power—God, the Divine, the Holy Spirit, Allah—whatever you call that spark of the Divine within that connects each of us to our Creator. I refer to it simply as "Spirit." When we find the spirit within, it changes us—we see, we experience, we understand—we realize that the spirit within, given to us by the God Source, is the true reality. We are Spirit, housed in a physical body. We are not our physical body, we are made up of all the qualities of our soul and our inner spirit. To understand how to communicate with the spirit world, we have to touch that spirit. When we do, we can recognize the same power in our spirit communicators.

Impact on Development

While developing your mediumship, it is common to experience a lack of confidence or a lack of trust in yourself. You wonder, "Is this the spirit world or is this my mind? Am I imagining this? Am I really a medium?" If you don't believe you are a medium, you haven't yet found the God source within. Once you have touched the spirit within you, the internal battle you have when receiving spirit world evidence will go away.

If you haven't experienced the mediumistic expression of your soul, it is difficult to be open to learning, and to accept constructive criticism. Remember me rolling my eyes and mumbling under my breath when my tutors said I needed to work on myself? They were right! I needed to build my relationship with the God power. The more inner work I did through prayer and meditation, the more I realized the importance of sitting in the power, walking meditations, and self-reflection. Prayer was woven into all I did.

Psychic Work

Discovering the true essence of your soul is a stepping stone to psychic work as well as mediumship work. The purpose of a psychic reading is to help your sitter improve their life, to give them direction and guidance. Psychic work involves blending with the soul power of your sitter, unfolding their soul's expression on a personal and spiritual level, and looking at their life story. We try to understand how the experiences they've been through have impacted their life. What has worked? What hasn't worked? What potential can they achieve within their soul?

Chances are you have been doing psychic readings for some time. You may use the Tarot, oracle cards, soul colors, or you may just link to the sitter's soul without "tools." It doesn't matter how you work, what matters is that you leave your sitter feeling uplifted and encouraged. Here is the structure I use in a psychic reading (with no spirit communication). I...

- blend with the sitter's soul.
- unfold their major life events, weaving in their character. How have the events impacted their life?
- unfold their life in the past year, in the past few months, and in the present.
- share with the sitter what I see as their soul's potential or true expression and / or their life's purpose, relating these to their past and current life.
- leave them with ideas on how to help themselves as they move forward.
- see possible outcomes in the future. Note: I never tell a sitter that what I see is an absolute. I say simply, "Here are some possibilities that may or may not happen."

As you have seen, it is important to create a solid foundation for your mediumship development. The first phase is to journey within to find the true expressions of your soul and create a relationship with the God power. The next phase is to develop your psychic faculties. As a medium you must take the time to work on this part of your soul's expression. Otherwise, when you begin to develop the mediumistic expression of your soul, you are going to hit some roadblocks. You may have heard the saying that "All mediums are psychic but not all psychics are mediums." That is true, and to be a good medium, you need good psychic skills.

Mediumship

Your goal as a medium is to surrender to the spirit world, allowing your spirit communicator to lead the way and unfold their life story. Three specific aspects of mediumship development will promote the expansion of your mediumistic skills: discipline, guidance, and finding your voice.

To surrender to the spirit world, first you need to focus the mind and discipline the self. Discipline is developed by sitting in meditation, by sitting in your own power, and by doing practical exercises.

In the early stages of your development, it is difficult to understand fully what is taking place within you and with the spirit world. So, second step, you need to find a teacher who can guide you, give you constructive feedback, and show you when you make mistakes. Your teacher cannot make you a medium, for as you have learned, the qualities you need to be a medium are already in your soul. Only you can allow those qualities to unfold and express themselves. Your teacher will give you insight on what you can do to move forward and let you know if what you are doing is working or not. If you find trusting spirit or going on a mind journey difficult, a teacher cannot give you a magic formula to make it happen. The work to be done is inner work—developing the power of your soul—and only you can do it.

The third aspect of mediumship that will help you shape your mediumistic talents is finding your voice. At this stage, you allow your soul and spirit team to move you forward. Once you have a solid foundation and you understand the unique expression of your soul, you are ready to go into the world, become your own teacher, and be your own medium. When that happens, you have become a professional medium!

Private Sittings

As noted earlier, throughout this book there are opportunities to expand your mediumship by doing the practice exercises, all of which will strengthen your private sittings and the platform work you do. I recommend practicing both the psychic and the mediumistic faculties with each of the exercises.

As you practice, set yourself a thirty-minute time frame in which to complete a reading. I was trained to not go beyond thirty minutes for a private sitting. Are you a little shocked to read that? Are you asking, "Only thirty minutes? Why?" Honestly, twenty minutes is plenty of time to give a mediumistic reading; the rest of the time can be used for a psychic connection or questions. If you decide to do a "little psychic" and a "little mediumistic" work in each sitting, it is better to begin with the psychic and then move to the spirit world. You will have clients who want "psychic only" or "mediumistic only"—and that is okay.

But again: make thirty minutes your goal. I know most clients want far more but it's hard to stay in your power for more than thirty minutes in one reading and if you go much beyond that, it becomes a struggle. It's taxing on the medium. It's always good to monitor your power during your reading. If it begins to drop and you are nearing the end of the session, it may be a good time to switch gears.

One of my tutors suggested that I never do more than four back-to-back mediumistic readings in one day. The reason? It drains your energy. It's too long to stay in your power properly. You can get away with doing more psychic readings because it's not as draining to your body. For example, if you do mediumistic readings at a psychic fair all day long, I'd ask you: "How many times did you drop into your psychic faculties? Was all the evidence coming from the psychic, not from the spirit world?"

In private sittings, on the other hand, it's okay to drop into the psychic—as long as you're aware of when it happens and you inform your sitter that the evidence is now coming from your soul, not from the spirit world. After all, you wouldn't want your sitter to think that "Granny said this or that," for example, when Granny was simply being an observer, not saying a word.

Dropping Your Power

How do you know when you've dropped into the psychic? It's a subtle shift in energy. A teacher can't teach you this; you have to feel it for yourself. With a psychic reading, your energy moves toward the sitter. In a mediumistic reading, your energy moves upward. One "red flag" that warns me of a shift in energy is when the evidence changes from being all about the spirit communicator (a mediumistic reading) to being all about the sitter (a psychic reading). A spirit communicator will mention a thing or two about the sitter—that's okay. But when the evidence suddenly becomes about the sitter; that's when I know I've gone psychic and I simply let the sitter know.

Structure of a Sitting

It's good to have structure with each sitting; it keeps you on track. Also, you'll want to have a set "introductory blurb" to share with your sitter before you begin each session. In that brief presentation, you'll want to outline how you work, how the sitting will unfold, and what (if any) specific regulations you need to abide by. For example, depending on where you live, your country may have guidelines on what you can say to your sitter. Perhaps you need to say that "This reading is for entertainment purposes only," or "I am sharing information only, what you choose to do with that information is your responsibility," or "Please consult with your medical practitioner if you require medical advice." I know that when I lived in the United Kingdom, there were specific procedures to follow. Check the laws and legislation in your country, and ensure you are doing everything legally.

Here is the structure I follow. I...
- introduce myself, smiling to put the sitter at ease.
- ask if they have ever had a reading before.
- explain what they can expect and to kindly give me "Yes," "No," or "I don't know" answers (nothing more).
- tell the sitter that there will be time for questions at the end of the session.
- read my disclaimer (see below).
- give a reading.
- ask if they have any questions before ending.
- thank them for the opportunity.

When I was practicing mediumship in the United Kingdom, having some sort of disclaimer was required. Here is an example of one I've used.

Readings are a form of experiment. No claims are made and results cannot be guaranteed. I am not a fortune teller. My aim is to try to give evidence of the survival of loved ones in the spirit world and to help you in your personal life. Spirit may include a glimpse of the recipient's life or a situation the individual(s) is experiencing at this particular time. Any life choices you make must be your own as you take full responsibility for your own life path. Always trust your own instincts first. Please understand that there are no guarantees of who will come through to communicate. If the loved one you wish to hear from does not come through, please know that it in no way indicates they do not love you. It simply means that today was not the right time or it could mean I am not the right medium for that particular loved one. If after ten minutes into the reading you are not satisfied, you may stop the reading for a full refund.

I've changed my disclaimer over the years. Now that I'm in the United States, I'm more relaxed. I've also had this waiver on my website. Some mediums ask their clients to sign a disclaimer (or check a box that they have read the disclaimer when booking online). You and your legal counsel will have to decide what will work for you. I urge you to ensure that you are covered in some way should an unhappy client file a complaint or worse, commence a lawsuit. Insurance is always a good idea and again, in some countries, it is mandatory. Please consult with your insurance adviser before starting your professional mediumship practice.

Contents of a Reading

There are many different methods and styles of mediumship, and not all of them are ideal. In the less-than-ideal approach, I've seen mediums begin by asking, "Is your mother in the spirit world?" If the answer is "Yes," the medium moves directly into explaining "Why your mother has come," or proceeds to give a message from the spirit communicator, without providing evidence to support that the medium does in fact have the sitter's mother. In such a case, the entire reading turns into a message for a sitter. If I went to a medium who worked this way, I would walk away wondering, "Did they really have my mother?" It isn't enough for us as mediums to say "I have your mother here." We have to give evidence that proves the mother is there, in that moment, for the sitter. I am a big skeptic—and if I'm skeptical, imagine what a non-medium might think.

In evidential mediumship, the medium gives evidence of survival to support their claim that (for example) "I have your mother with me." We want the sitter to know, without a doubt, that we have their loved one with us by giving examples: How they lived their life, what their personality was like, what they did for their career, and so forth. It is okay to give a message at the end of an evidential reading if you feel a need to do so, but it isn't necessary—sometimes the evidence contains the message; the sitter knows what it means but the medium may not. I've had clients come to me with specific questions and without me knowing it, their questions were answered in the reading. At the end, I've asked, "Do you have any questions?" Often, the sitter has just smiled and said, "You've already answered them." That shows the intelligence of the spirit world!

The following guidelines are for both private sittings and working on platform doing gallery demonstrations.

o   The medium's goal is to weave the story of a life –
   •   If it's a psychic reading, it is the story of the sitter.
   •   If it's a mediumistic reading, it's the story of the spirit communicator.
o   Aspects of a spirit communicator's life –
   •   This could include (but is not limited to) aspects of personality, where the person lived, hobbies, career, relationship to the sitter, or how they passed.
o   Shared experiences –
   •   This would include memories shared with the sitter.
o   Encouragement to sitter –
   •   This encouragement can come through during the reading or at the end in the form of a message. If we surrender to the spirit world, the communicator will artfully weave the message they want to give to their loved one through the story being told. If this hasn't happened, leave the sitter with a few words of encouragement.
o   Connection in spirit world –
   •   People in this world always want to know if, after passing, their loved one found Grandma, Uncle Bob, or a beloved pet when they got to the spirit world. So, share a bit of what their loved one is doing in the spirit world.
o   Closing comments –
   •   Wrap up your reading with an uplifting comment, a few words of reassurance, or inspiration for your sitter. Leaving your sitter feeling supported and empowered can make all the difference.

Platform Demonstrations

"Platform demonstrations" are the same as "a gallery reading" here in the United States. Most of my training was standing on a platform, working in front of an audience. For a shy person, I'm surprised to say it is my favorite way to work. I love the challenge of never knowing how the audience will react. I'm astonished, for example, at seeing the intelligence of the spirit world when they take me to "The fifth row from the back, three seats over," directly to a loved one, when there are 100 people in the audience. It amazes me every time.

The contents of a demonstration reading are the same as in a private sitting—but there are a few key differences:

- First, you only have seven to ten minutes, not thirty minutes, to get a demonstration reading done.
- Second, it's imperative that you identify your recipient in the first few minutes.
- Third, while you are giving your reading to the recipient, you have to keep the rest of the audience interested.

We are always aware of our sitter's needs, making sure they are happy, and the reading is fulfilling their expectations (as it should be in all readings). What about the needs of the spirit communicator? Imagine you are in the spirit world and you've just learned that there are mediums on Earth who could help you communicate with your loved one. Imagine how exciting that must be for them to be able to come and say "I love you" one more time. Now imagine they have one shot to get this right. There's a sense of urgency to say all they need to say in a short amount of time.

On the platform, as noted, the medium has seven to ten minutes to make it happen for the communicator. You can't spend the entire time locating your recipient, so you have two options. You can throw strong evidence out to everyone and see how many hands go up or you can trust the spirit communicator to pull your energy to a specific place in the audience and narrow it down quickly. To help you determine which method will work best in any given circumstance, there are two rules. When the first few pieces of evidence are "Strong" pieces that few people would understand, you can throw those out to the audience. Examples of this type of evidence would be a person who passed by being trampled by a bull, someone who was a professional opera singer, someone who taught in a school for the deaf, or someone who worked alongside the president of the United States. This type of evidence will narrow down the recipients in the audience fast. That said, I caution you about going to your recipient before giving any evidence. Skeptical persons in the audience will think it's a setup. They will say you knew you were going to that person, that the evidence was planned. Another cautionary note is that finding your recipient first creates an easier opportunity for you to drop into the psychic, especially if there is no spirit communicator with you when you begin. So, be mindful of these two pitfalls.

"General" evidence is evidence that makes us go directly to a recipient—or at least makes us go to the general area they are seated in. I usually work this way because I tend to give the essence of the communicator first before going into specific evidence. Physical descriptions, clothing, personality, or typical daily routines (like "She was a homemaker") all constitute "general information." If you threw this evidence out to the audience, more than half of the participants would raise their hands. Then you'd have to sift through, narrowing down who your spirit communicator wants to speak to. Meanwhile, the spirit communicator is getting anxious because they know you only have three minutes left, they have a lot to say, and you've lost the audience's attention. Yikes!

The last things to consider when doing platform demonstrations is your audience and your stage presence. The role of the medium is to take command of the audience: exuding confidence, speaking loudly and clearly, and controlling whom in the audience you will work with. I would urge anyone who has limited experience in working with an audience or speaking in front of large groups of people to seek out classes in public speaking. They will teach you all the tips of engaging the audience, your body posture, voice projection, voice enunciation, and eye contact. All of these things are a must to hold the audience's attention. (Check with your local Toastmasters organization—these classes are generally free or given at a nominal charge.)

When it comes to public speaking, I had things pointed out to me that I never imagined I needed to correct. For example, my long hair blocked the audience's view of my face and I said "um" after every word. These little habits are annoying to the audience and don't present a professional image. There is a lot to think about when it comes to stage presence and a little help from someone knowledgeable is a good idea.

Touching the Spirit Within

If there is just one thing I can leave you with as you move forward in this book, it is the importance of touching the spirit within. There is a difference between what you think you are all about and actually experiencing or touching your true essence. Work toward that experience.

Your life will change for the better when you go through this on the mental, physical, and spiritual levels.

In this chapter, I have presented an overview of several important topics in order to give you "a heads-up" about what is to come and to get you started in your practice exercises as you develop the characteristics and structured routines of a polished, professional medium. I know you may have established your methodology for your readings already. I share mine with you to provide another potential way of doing things. Find what works for you. Remember, our goal as mediums is to connect pieces of evidence together to create a beautiful story honoring the life of the spirit communicator. The type and quality of evidence you give during a reading will make all the difference.

In the chapters to follow, I will go in more detail about these subjects. As I mentioned earlier, I hope you'll do all the exercises in the book repeatedly for the next few years. Practice makes perfect!

Exercises:

On my website, you can download two checklists to use with any of the exercises. One is for a private sitting, the other is for when you practice in front of a group, small or large. I've included a few extra components that you can have your practice sitters check off on a "Completed" list, which will help to ensure that you cover these aspects in each of your sittings. If you find the checklists include more detail than you are accustomed to, remember, you are planting new seeds to nurture and improve upon. We all have to start somewhere! Do what you can for now. If you continue to practice, in a year from now, you will see improvement.

There are also checklists as well as video tutorials included as part of the Medium's Club Membership on my website. If you join the club, before you begin the exercises in this book, go to my website to get your copy ... and be sure to watch the videos of me demonstrating how to do each exercise. I hope you enjoy them!

Recordings

All through my training, I recorded my readings, reviewed the recordings, and analyzed my results. I cannot say it was fun. I dreaded it. But it was a powerful tool and I'm grateful I did these tasks. As time went on, I could see my growth and what I needed to strengthen. The best part was watching a reading from a year earlier and comparing it to a current reading. It restored my faith and belief in myself as a medium.

So, I urge you to record all your practice readings. Save them in a special folder with the date and the type of exercise labeled clearly. As you move along on your spiritual path, practice the same exercises, and record them again. Compare the current video to the first one. See how much you've grown!

EXERCISE 1

Opening, Introduction, and Disclaimer

Objective:

Create an opening introduction and a disclaimer if needed.

Materials Needed:

Journal.

Procedure:

Think about what you would like to use as an opening statement, to convey to the sitter or the audience information about how the reading or demonstration will unfold and what they can expect. I suggest doing two, one for a private sitting and one for an audience.

Table #3: Possible Private Sitting Introduction/Possible Introduction for an Audience

Expectations	
Possible Private Sitting Introduction	**Possible Introduction for an Audience**
• Greet your sitter warmly to put them at ease.	• Smile, introduce who you are, where you are from, and why you are here.
• If your country has specific guidelines, include them.	• Give directions of "Yes," "No," and "I don't know."

• No guarantees of who comes through	• Explain if you are going to go direct, throw it out, or both.
• Reassurance: If desired loved one doesn't come through, it does not mean they don't love the sitter.	• Ask the audience to speak up when asked to respond.
• Results cannot be guaranteed.	• Explain briefly if you plan to work mediumistically, psychically, or both. I do not suggest explaining which clairs you use. Most people won't understand the terminology. Keep it simple.
• Follow your instincts on any advice given.	
• After ten minutes, if not happy, they can have a refund	

I suggest writing these introductory statements out on a card. Practice saying them as you begin a private sitting or a group reading to get yourself in the habit. Eventually, you won't need the cards, it will be automatic.

Exercises 2 and 3

Using a Checklist for a Private Sitting or Platform Reading

Objective:

The aim of the exercise is to bring your awareness to having a structure for a private reading and a platform reading.

Type of Reading:

I recommend doing all these readings as one-to-one sittings, both psychically and mediumistically, to get a good grasp on how to bring it all together. You may practice them in group or gallery settings using mediumistic faculties if you can get extra people or are working in a circle. One-to-one sittings are fifteen to thirty minutes long for the purpose of a practice exercise. Gallery style readings are seven to ten minutes long.

Materials Needed:

- Device to record your reading.
- Journal.
- Handout: Structure of a Private Reading Checklist (Free download on my website).
- Handout: Structure of a Platform Demonstration Checklist (Free download on my website)

- View Videos: (optional) Structure of a Private Reading and Structure of a Platform Reading

Structure of a Private Reading and Platform/Gallery Reading
Number of Participants:
- Two or more.

Table #4: Expectations: Private Sitting and Platform/Gallery Reading

Expectations Private Sitting and Platform/Gallery Reading		
Medium's Role	**Recipient's Role**	**Audience's Role**
• Give your introduction. • Get into your power. • Set your intention. • Do your reading. • Close. *For platform only:* • After the first contact, begin a second contact.	• The sitter is the time keeper. Please let the medium know when they have exceeded their time. • Feedback should consist of "Yes," "No," "I don't know," or "I am not sure." • No additional feedback is necessary. • Using the checklist, record the evidence given. Be honest.	• Allow the medium to be in control. If they choose to work with someone else, do not interrupt. • Give answers of "Yes," "No," or "I don't know," only. • Do not give feedback to the medium demonstrating after their reading is finished. Wait until the group discusses the process to give any additional feedback.

Procedures:

1. Set your intent.
2. Hit "Record" on your phone or recorder.
3. Do the reading.
4. Stop recording.

Discussion with Group or Partner About the Process or Exercise:
- Using the checklist as a reference, discuss with the sitter how the reading went.
- In what ways was this exercise similar to how you have been working?
- How was the exercise different than your normal way of working?
- What aspects came to you easily?
- Which aspects did you find more challenging?
- Moving forward, what goals can you set for yourself?

Journal:

- Reflect on how you feel about your reading today. Write down your thoughts.
- Share any emotions or struggles that may have come up.
- What were your strengths? Where did you have challenges? Write these down.
- What was your "gold nugget," the best bit of the reading? Write it down.
- Close your eyes. Take a few deep breaths. Ask your soul, "What wisdom do you want to leave with me today?" Wait for the answer to come—start writing.

To see things in the seed, that is genius.

—Lao Tzu

Chapter 4

"Planting Seeds"

"I'm sitting in the power but nothing is happening." Have you ever said those words? "I'm doing the exercises but it doesn't go the way it should." Is this you? "I practice all the time but I can't see any progress." Have you made statement like, "I think spirit blocked me," or "The sitter is blocking me?" Most mediums have these or similar thoughts at some point. It's okay. We live in a world of instant results. Unfortunately, navigating the mediumship path isn't instant. It's true that we are able to connect with the spirit world most of the time but there are also times when we can feel as if we've hit a wall. Despite doing everything our teachers are teaching us, nothing seems to get us past that wall.

It's easy to get caught up in outcomes, and to look forward to our "prize"—that moment we reach "professional medium" status—and to miss what's going on behind the scenes.

So, what is going on behind the scenes? What must occur so we can finally say, "I'm a working medium?" It's human nature for us to build a box to sit inside of. We fill that box with ideas of "how things will play out." But, in the real world, things don't always go according to plan. When things go awry, we get agitated, we point fingers, we blame outside influences—and we miss the big picture.

What expectations have you placed in your comfortable mediumship box? Do you expect your mediumship to blossom overnight? You have all the tools you need, right? So, why aren't things moving forward more quickly? I believe we must climb out of that box, move beyond it, throw away our preconceived ideas. If I've learned anything in mediumship, it's that things never go the way I thought they were going to go. Never.

When you are sitting in the power and nothing is happening, what do you think the spirit world is doing? You are in your power—and it's a perfect opportunity for the spirit world to come in and work with you behind the scenes. Trust spirit to be there—always.

I sat with my guide for a year but he would not speak to me. It was like a great standoff between him and me. After about a year, finally he began to answer my many questions. I know now that in that year a bond was forming. I could feel the shifts within myself, especially as I began to heal. Trust that your development is moving exactly as spirit intends.

I know what you're thinking: "But what about the exercises I've done over and over?" I wondered the same thing. We're no different. Here's what I learned on my journey.

Recall that earlier I referred to mediumship as a process of planting seeds. Whether you are a seasoned medium working with clients or a medium-in-training, you are sowing seeds. Seasoned mediums plant seeds for their clients to take with them when they leave; training mediums plant seeds for their own development. The first time I tried a new exercise, for example, I planted a seed. Each time I repeated that exercise, I was nurturing that seed. I was, in a sense, watering it and giving it sunlight. As I worked diligently and patiently, that seed sprouted, burst through the topsoil, and grew into a strong, tall plant. As mediums, we nurture our soul's progression and the awakening that is occurring within us. We become stronger and better with each attempt—and our learning takes place in layers. In the first layer, we plant the seed by doing the exercise. With the second layer, we do the exercise again, and take in a little more understanding. For the third layer, we go a little further, we grasp a little more. We continue like this and with each attempt, our understanding deepens—until we are able to do every exercise with ease.

Be gentle with yourself. Remember, mediumship is not an acorn. It's the whole oak tree.

Pace yourself, nurture the acorn. Growing takes time, so be patient—it takes a while to allow the roots of the oak to grow deep and strong.

Trusting in spirit was my oak tree. I nurtured it for a long time: years. Some skills I learned were like that tiny acorn—I caught on fast. Other skills needed time. I had to keep working, knowing that one day I would stand tall, roots firmly planted, tough, resilient, and enduring. No matter what storms might come, my mature oak tree will hold fast and remain upright.

As we nurture the seeds we plant through the exercises we do, we create new ways for the spirit world to work through us. We strengthen the spiritual faculties we came here with and allow our souls to rise in wondrous ways. Why limit what we can offer to the spirit world?

A New Seed, A New Strength

Early in my development, clairvoyance was my only tool. I saw everything: the movies in my head were my best friends. One day, I went to a workshop at the Arthur Findlay College conducted by a tutor who wouldn't let us use clairvoyance. I panicked. I struggled the entire day using my clairsentience. I had never even heard of clairsentience. It wasn't easy. Reading after reading, I tried desperately to use this new clair. I was frustrated and embarrassed. To make matters worse, I had to give the tutor a reading in front of my peers. It was one of the most difficult days in my training. On the flip side, it ended up being one of the most influential days in all of my studies. It just goes to show that if you want to make massive gains, you have to take risks. You have to sweat it out. From that day forward, I no longer received clairvoyant images. The movies in my head were gone and I was forced to use the only other clair I now knew: clairsentience. This continued for over a hard but empowering year. My clairsentience became so strong, I moved into the very essence of my spirit communicators, something I had never done. It was so exciting!

Many of my tutors had me do exercises using clairvoyant images—déjà vu all over again. Every time I tried to receive an image from a spirit communicator, I crashed and burned. It was my introduction to what I call "the mediumship roller coaster." Up, down. Highs, lows. The struggle was real. I asked my guide, "Would it be possible to start using images again?" No response. But, every once in a while, an image would slip through. It was like a teaser: "Remember when you always got images?" Then the clairvoyance was gone again, without even saying goodbye.

I continued to ask my guide, "Can we bring back the images for the exercises?" Finally, a response. He posed this question: "Why do you ask for only one image at a time for a particular exercise?" That stopped me in my tracks. Good question. Why? Was it because the exercise required one or two images only? Possibly. As I reflected back to the early days when I saw movies in my head, I realized my guide was right. My request was wrong. I didn't want an image here or there to get through an exercise. I wanted my movies back. My next chat with my guide, I changed my request: "May I please have my movies back?"

It wasn't long before I began to have mini-movies while I worked. They still weren't the same caliber they'd been in the early years but I was grateful to have them easing back into my readings. I spoke with a tutor about this. She explained it was time for me to learn how to use my clairsentience *with* my clairvoyance. I learned that evidence passes through the clairsentience first and then makes it way to the other clairs. The key is to allow yourself to feel the evidence with the clairsentience and then allow that feeling to bubble up to the third eye to form an image.

I share this story with you because as mediums we can't be complacent about the type of evidence we bring. I would have been happy working from nothing but images—I'd been successful working in that way. But had I stayed with only clairvoyance, I would have missed out on the incredible evidence that was brought forward in different ways.

Spiritual Tools

I believe that we all come to this world with a cache of spiritual jewels locked inside us to help us on our journey. These tools are held within our soul and spirit just waiting to awaken. For some people these tools begin to unlock naturally at an early age. Others may experience a traumatic event that jars them to the core of their being—and then that treasure chest opens. For others, a near death experience (NDE) can do the same thing. It doesn't matter how your awakening begins. What matters is what you decide to do once this awakening of your soul occurs and your spiritual tools are revealed to you.

Your spiritual tools are a part of you, a part of your soul. As they draw close, they allow you to become aware of the spirit world. You'll know, for example, that your psychic senses are awakening when you get goosebumps and feel as if there is an unseen spirit around you. Trust these feelings. It's time to nurture your psychic senses—your clairs—so they can flourish. There are three main clairs we use when working psychically:

- *clairvoyance*, which means seeing images,
- *clairsentience*, which is using the sense of feeling, and
- *claircognizance*, which is clear knowing.

We will explore these clairs later. The best way to nurture your clairs (as I've noted earlier) is to go within, learn about your own spirit or soul, and heal the scars your soul carries. As you move along your mediumship path, you'll discover more tools and spiritual faculties, and as you develop these, you'll open up new clairs.

You may find that as you progress, your strengths are different from other mediums'—and that's okay. The goal is to open up to all your clairs and use them. Clairvoyance, clairsentience, and clairaudience are the most prevalent clairs for most mediums but you may discover that different clairs are stronger for you.

Spirit's Needs

As you watch other mediums work, you'll notice that everyone has their own unique style. Their personalities come to the fore, their delivery of evidence varies, and how they work with each recipient is different. While some of their methods will be similar to others', most mediums will have their own "special stamp." It's no different in the spirit world. Your spirit clients will each have their own unique way of working—and they will each have their strengths and weaknesses. Just because they are in the spirit world doesn't mean they can work "your way." You may have a spirit communicator who works well with clairvoyant images and who can take you on mind journeys. Your next communicator may need to work through your clairsentience; the next may use a combination of all the clairs. So, if you have developed only one clair and that's not the clair your spirit communicator can work with well, how will that affect your reading? You may make it to the end—but was it the best reading you could have offered? Wouldn't it be better to meet the spirit world halfway? We cannot expect the spirit world to do all the work for us. The more we have to offer the spirit world, the easier it will be to work with them—and they with us.

Foundations for Mediumship

Recall that earlier we discussed mediumship development as the planting and nurturing of seeds. Plant an acorn and you'll grow an oak tree. The longer you nurture that acorn, the stronger your oak tree will become. So, be patient. Go easy on yourself and persist. Here's a cap up of all the ways you can nurture your oak tree:
- Sit in the power often.
- Sit with your guide once or twice a week.

- Do exercises to strengthen your psychic faculties.
- Do exercises to strengthen your mediumship faculties.
- Develop all of your clairs.
- Do soul work to heal.

To be a strong professional medium, we must exercise our spiritual faculties and create a healthy, healed soul. The more we put into our development, the stronger we'll be in our work. It's that simple, guys. I learned this "soul work lesson" at the gym. Right after a divorce, I joined a body building school. You know the story—a single gal must have a hot body to boot scoot around the dance floor! The owner of the gym was a world champion body builder who stressed the importance of working the whole body, not just the areas you want to change. Many of the men at this school ignored his valuable advice, focusing on upper body strength only, neglecting the lower half of their body. Over time, they had nice bulging muscles in their arms and chests but when you saw their legs, you saw two twigs holding up all those muscles on top. The lower and upper halves of their bodies were disproportionate. These men thought their legs were strong enough and didn't need exercise, so while their upper bodies grew bigger and stronger, their legs stayed the same. Their thinking led them astray.

Let's not fall into this line of thinking with our mediumship. Mediumship development is like going to a spiritual gym. To have a strong, healthy body, you must exercise and eat healthy foods. To be a strong, versatile medium, you must develop all your clairs. So, do all the exercises in this book, even if you crash and burn over and over (like I did). Eventually you will get there!

Your Team

Are you ready? Let's start by acknowledging our guides, helpers, and inspirers from the spirit world. Take time to get to know them. Chat with them daily, and even if you don't get any feedback, trust that they are listening. One day, the answers will come. Your spirit guides, helpers, and inspirers are an integral part of your team. You wouldn't start a business partnership without knowing your business partners well, would you? Your partnership with your spirit world team is no different. I know two of my guides very well. I know that the others are there, listening and guiding me, so I always include them. I urge you to get to know your main guide well. Treat them like they are your best friend for life ... they are!

Building Your Foundation

In this chapter, we have covered how to build a solid foundation for your mediumship work. A cap up: Pace yourself. Be patient. Persevere. Allow your spiritual faculties to flourish naturally. Remember, the learning curve for mediums is for life. Your talents will grow, develop, and blossom at just the right speed for you.

EXERCISE 1

Let it Flow

Objective:

To create a nice flow in your delivery.

Type of Reading:

I recommend doing all these readings as one-to-one sittings, both psychically and mediumistically, to get a good grasp on how to bring it all together. If you can get extra people or you are working in a circle, you may practice these exercises in group or gallery settings using mediumistic faculties. One-to-one sittings are fifteen to thirty minutes long for the purpose of a practice exercise. Gallery style readings are seven to ten minutes long.

Materials Needed:

- Device to record your reading.
- Journal.
- Blindfold (Optional).
- Video – Let It Flow (Optional).

Number of Participants:

- Four or more.

Table #5: Expectations: Let it Flow

Expectations: Let it Flow	
Medium's Role	**Recipient's Role**
• Use a blindfold or sit with your back to the recipient, with your eyes closed.	• The sitter is the time keeper. Please let the medium know when they have exceeded their time.
• Give a reading.	• No additional feedback is necessary.
• Stay in your power after receiving a "No."	• Once the medium is ready to begin, quietly go and sit behind or in front of them, ensuring the medium does not know the identity of the sitter.
	• The recipient is to sit in silence and give no responses.
	• Tap the medium on the shoulder or knee to let them know you are there.
	• At the end of the reading, tap the medium to let them know their time is up and quietly move away from the medium.
	• When all readings are completed, let the medium know they can remove their blindfold.

Procedures:

1. The first reading should be psychic.
2. Take a five-minute break. Then those who were a sitter first will take a seat with the blindfold on, and those who were the medium first will go and sit quietly behind or in front of the new medium.

3. Repeat Steps above.
4. There is no need for sitter feedback or for the medium to know whom they are reading. (See below for explanation.)

Repeat the same procedure for the mediumistic reading after all participants have given a psychic reading.

Keep Calm and Carry On

Objective:

The aim is to stay in your power after receiving a "No" from the sitter.

Type of Reading:

I recommend doing all these readings as one-to-one sittings to get a good grasp on how to bring it all together. If you can get extra people or are working in a circle, you may practice them in group or gallery settings. One-to-one settings are fifteen to thirty minutes long. Gallery style readings are seven to ten minutes long.

Materials Needed:

- Device to record your reading.
- Journal.
- Video – Keep Calm and Carry On (Optional).

Number of Participants:

- Four or more.

Table #6: Expectations: Keep Calm and Carry On

Expectations: Keep Calm and Carry On	
Medium's Role	**Recipient's Role**
• Use a blindfold or sit with your back to the recipient with eyes closed. • Give a reading. • Allow the evidence to come and give it freely without thinking or pausing. • At the end, wait for the sitter to move away.	• Once the medium is ready to begin, go and sit behind or in front of them quietly, ensuring that the medium does not know the identity of the sitter. • The sitter is the time keeper. • The sitter will give one tap on shoulder or knee for a "Yes" answer, two taps for "No," and three taps if they aren't sure or don't know. • No words are spoken. • Tap the medium on the shoulder or knee to let them know you are there. • At the end of the reading, tap the medium to let them know their time is up and move away from the medium quietly. • When all readings are completed, let the medium know they can remove their blindfold.

Procedures:

1. Medium gets settled first, wearing a blindfold.
2. The sitter or recipient sits quietly behind or in front of the medium. Tap the medium on the knee or shoulder to let them know you are there.
3. Medium connects, begins the reading.
4. Sitter taps medium when time is expired and moves away quietly.
5. Take a five-minute break. Then those who were a sitter first will take a seat with the blindfold on, and those who

were the medium first will go and sit quietly behind or in front of the new medium.
6. Repeat steps above.
7. For mediums, there is no need to know who the sitter was, and for sitters there is no need for feedback.

Mediums tend to practice with the same mediums over and over. If you get detailed feedback each time, you open possibilities of evidence from past readings coming into your mind in future readings. Not knowing if you are right or wrong (or who your recipient was) is a great way for mediums to keep past readings for the same recipient from coming into memory on subsequent readings.

I'm not saying that you should do this always but mixing it up and having a nice balance of no feedback versus a small amount of feedback is a nice way to practice. Also, I caution you on giving too much feedback. Keep it simple and brief. In my training, we were only allowed to say "Yes," "No," or "I don't know." If the evidence was partly correct, then we gave a "No." Only evidence that was 100% correct got a "Yes."

Discussion with Group or Partner About the Process or Exercise:
- What emotions came forward with not knowing who sat behind you?
- What was the level of difficulty working in this way? Was it harder or easier not getting responses?
- What areas gave you the most difficulty?
- Were you able to keep the information going without too many pauses? Why or why not?
- How did you handle the "No's?"
- Did you keep going?
- Could you feel your energy drop?

- What was your "gold nugget," the part that you are most proud of, or your best piece of evidence?
- What is one area you'd like to chat with your spirit team about, to get help on or to gain understanding about?

Journal:

- Reflect on how you feel about your reading today and write down your thoughts.
- Share any emotions or struggles that came up.
- What were your strengths? Where did you have challenges? Write these down.
- What was your "gold nugget," the best bit of the reading? Write it down.
- What seed did you plant today and how do you plan to nourish it in the future?
- Close your eyes. Take a few deep breaths. Ask your soul, "What wisdom do you want to leave with me today?" Wait for the answer to come—start writing.

*The tiny seed knew that in order to grow it needed
to be dropped in dirt, covered in darkness,
and struggle to reach the light.*

—Sandra Kring

CHAPTER 5

"BEYOND YOUR COMFORT ZONE"

Working with a List

In a small-town development circle I once sat in, I learned to use a "spirit world check list." The list required mediums to get physical descriptions, names, dates, clothing, how the communicator died, and more. But it didn't feel natural to me to be "interviewing" my sitter's loved ones. It made me "get in my head"—I'm sure the spirit communicator was wondering, "What is this woman doing?"

After circle, I often felt like a failure because I was unable to bring through the evidence my tutor had expected from me. I would go home, sit on the floor, close my eyes, and take a few moments to sit in silence. One day, my guide came and sat with me; I could see him clearly in my mind's eye. He looked at me; our eyes seemed to lock. Whenever this happened, it was as if I could see into his soul and he could see into mine. The love I felt emanating from him always brought me to tears. Somewhere deep within me, I knew this man, there was a connection between us.

As we sat together on the floor, I could hear him speaking—not like I hear people speak sitting across the table from me, but with thoughts and images. Looking into his eyes, I knew exactly what he wanted me to understand. His thoughts floated through my mind.

He asked, "Why are you upset?" He pointed out that the evidence I'd brought through that night was good evidence about my spirit communicator. I'd made a connection. There was no need to be upset.

I said, "But I didn't do as the tutor asked. I didn't bring through how they'd died, didn't give a special date ... a birthday, an anniversary, the date of passing, their age."

He knew I thought I had failed.

In my mind's eye, I felt him place his hand on mine. A shiver ran through me. In his eyes, I saw how proud of me he was for the work I had done that night. He smiled reassuringly and asked, "What would want to hear your Dad say to you if he were to come through in a reading?"

I wasn't sure what he meant so I decided to hold on to it and give it a good think. He smiled, patted my hand, and was gone. I sat on the floor, thoughts racing through my head, trying to make sense of all that had transpired. It wasn't until months later that I realized: If Dad came through in a reading for me and gave the day of his passing, I might not be able to confirm the evidence. I don't remember the exact date—or his exact age. My parents never told us their ages when we were growing up, nor did we give much thought to birthday celebrations. So, I didn't pay attention to those details.

What I remember is the phone call I received to let me know Dad was en route to hospital. I remember the long walk from the hospital parking lot to the emergency room entrance, seeing my brother just outside the entrance embracing my mom, the deafening silence of the two-minute walk to reach them despite the sounds of a jackhammer pounding away a few feet to my right, the feeling of knowing I was too late, that I would never be able to say "I love you" to Dad again. That is what is etched forever into my memory of that day. That's what I remember ... not the date, not the time, not his age. This was a profound realization. I finally saw what my guide had wanted me to see. In that moment, my mediumship changed. I walked away from the "list of evidence" I was supposed to get in every reading. I began to allow the spirit communicator to share whatever evidence they chose. The spirit communicator knows their loved one. I do not.

Who am I to demand certain types evidence?

When I allowed the communicator to share as they wished, I noticed that their life story began to unfold. The recipient smiled and nodded as their loved one took them down memory lane. I knew the communicator was happy sharing the memories, I could feel their joy as they watched their loved one. The tug-of-war between myself and the spirit world had ended, because I was no longer demanding types of evidence.

In my opinion, this is what mediumship is about—reconnecting the discarnate spirit with the incarnate here on earth, giving those who are still here peace of mind knowing that their loved one is still part of their life. It's about allowing the discarnate to come and say, "I love you, I'm still very much alive. We'll be together again."

It's not always about a list of facts, like what they look like or what they are wearing. Their age isn't important, neither is how they died. There are exceptions to bringing through this type of evidence of course, and later in this chapter we'll get into when it's a good idea to tap into "the list" and how you can use it to your advantage. But in most readings, the "things on the list" aren't the most important information.

Physical Descriptions

It's easy to fall into the trap of stereotyping those who come to us from the spirit world. We can see them in our mind's eye and based on what we see, we assume details about their character, life, or where they lived. We are really careful of this because what appears in a clairvoyant image doesn't always show the true story.

Working in this way is the norm in the early stages of our mediumship development. We are happy to receive any information and we give exactly what we receive—we see an image, we describe it, our mind comes in, puts its own spin on things, and interprets the evidence. The sooner we move beyond this method, however, the easier it will be to master the next stage. If we wait too long, there'll be more work to do to break the habits we have formed. When we move away from describing exactly what we see, we move into the energy of the image—and we discover the hidden story. This in turn opens up the other clairs—we feel emotions, we hear sounds or words, we even taste and smell things. All the other clairs enhance the evidence and a story begins to unfold.

In the early part of my development, I did a reading which taught me how to let go and let the spirit communicator's story unfold. I brought through a grandmother, Nan, whose appearance was typical of women her age. She had short white hair and felt warm and cuddly. She was nurturing, loved her family, and dedicated her life to them. Of course, all of this is general information that most people can take about their grandmother. As I moved past the first evidence, I became aware of her life being anything but ordinary. I was aware of her husband, whom the sitter called Opa, serving in WWII. I knew they were both connected to the war, I was aware of medals of valor given to her husband. I became aware of a war injury her husband had, which caused problems with one of his legs. Memories of them in their younger years came to me: I saw them dancing, having a great time together, sharing family gatherings where there was singing and dancing. They took me to their house, showed me what life was like for them, showed me road signs written in two different languages, Welsh and German. It turned out that Nan had lived in Wales and Opa in Germany—that's why I saw the road signs in different languages. The grandmother showed me a pearl necklace that was near and dear to her that was now in her daughter's care. As I worked with this grandmother and grandfather, their love story began to unfold. They met while the grandfather, Opa, was a prisoner of war in a prison in Wales. The grandmother, Nan, would walk along the fence of the prison and see Opa. She would stop to talk. It wasn't long and they began to fall in love. Family and friends accused her of being a traitor and said she was crossing the enemy line by seeing this boy in prison. Opa would tunnel under the fence to see her at night. On a few occasions, he was caught and put in solitary confinement. He didn't care. They were in love.

While he was on a day pass to leave the prison, Nan and Opa got married. Sadly, Opa had to return to the prison immediately and was not allowed to spend his wedding night with his bride. It wasn't until a year later that they released him. They defied the odds, went against their families' wishes ... and went on to have six children. On their sixtieth wedding anniversary, the Queen of England gave them the incredible honor of congratulating them on their true love story.

Nan had an extraordinary story to tell. For me, the lesson from this reading was to move beyond the physical description and stereotypes, and to allow the story to unfold so the spirit communicators could bring their story to life.

What an amazing story! The recipient had filled in bits and pieces of this evidence for me but I didn't care. I was excited that I let go and let spirit lead the way. As time went on, I learned to fill in the gaps and my recipients no longer needed to do that for me. Finally, I saw what my guide had been trying to point out to me that day when he'd asked, "What would you want to hear from your dad?"

Let's take a look now at how we can begin to see descriptions of spirit communicators in a new way.

Exercise

Seeing Grandmas in a New Way

Take a look at the chart below. Notice the use of typical words a medium might use to describe grandmothers from a clairvoyant image.

Table #7: Physical Descriptions

Physical Descriptions				
Spirit Communicator	**Hair**	**Physical Features**	**Character or surroundings**	**Clothing/ accessories**
	White or gray Short Maybe a little Curly	Full cheeks Wrinkles Sun Spots	Fun	Big hat Glasses
	Gray Short Waves or curls	Wrinkles Oval-shaped Round figure	Reader Sitting at table Shopping Likes to dress nice Maybe has money	Glasses Earrings Newspaper Hat with brooch Plaid skirt Button shirt Dress coat
	Short Gray Curls or waves	Wrinkles Deep set eyes Thin	Looks kind	Sweater with button shirt underneath Glasses
	Gray Short Straight	Wrinkles Round belly 5' 7"	Wall phone Simple furnishings Not a lot of money	Cotton gown/ dress with flowers Glasses

All of these pieces of evidence would work well in a private sitting. But let's think about working with an audience. Most elderly people have similar physical characteristics and many have led similar lives. If you use general descriptions, you will have many hands go up to take the evidence, creating a problem as you sort out the real recipient. Physical descriptions can make or break a reading. It's a bit tricky ... for example, if you say 5'7" and they were 5'8" some audience members or sitters won't take the evidence. It will throw them off and they will think you don't have their loved one.

We are careful when giving physical descriptions, as it is easy to get it wrong (or not exactly right), causing your recipient to say "No." Think about it ... how many times in your life do you change your hairstyle, hair color, and clothing style? Your appearance is always changing to reflect the fashions of the time. The spirit communicator can present themselves to you in any way they choose and their loved one may not recognize what they are showing you.

Too many times I've seen a recipient refuse to take a loved one because the medium said they had blonde hair when their true hair color was brown or the medium got their age or height wrong. Recipients will hold on to what you said.

Let's take a look at the evidence in the chart above. If you throw out to the audience, "I have an elderly woman, possibly a grandmother, with short gray hair and glasses," three-fourths of your audience will raise their hands. You will lose a few hands if you add "She wore unusual hats," or "She was a lot of fun," or "She dressed nicely and loved to shop" but you will still have hands raised, with members of your audience hoping you have *their* grandmother.

This teaches us to move into the energy of the clairvoyant image. What story is hidden behind the image? Nan from the reading above had short gray hair and glasses. Imagine how the reading would have gone, if I had left it at that and not moved into the image to see what was hidden? I wouldn't have uncovered that amazing love story and touched the life of my sitter.

We must train ourselves to move beyond physical descriptions. Dig a little deeper, learn about the spirit communicator's life. It's their life and their memories that will be most important to their loved ones. That said, don't get me wrong, there is also a time and place for using physical descriptions.

When Descriptions Work

If you have a communicator who is unusually tall or short, it will make it easier to find your recipient. Similarly, if you have a communicator with prominent scars, tattoos, physical limitations, or even missing limbs, it becomes more relevant because not many people in your audience will be able to accept that specific evidence. Sometimes you will have a spirit communicator who dressed in a certain way that made them stand out in a crowd. For example, if you have a man who wore bold plaid pants every day, used a rope for a belt, and paired his pants with a bright, flowery Hawaiian shirt, point that out. Not many people would know someone in the spirit world who fit that description!

I know a woman who always wore a funny hat, with many different types of decorative pins, and her outfits often didn't match. Her fashion sense was so bad that her granddaughter would inspect her outfits and make her change before going out in public. It was the running family joke to guess what

Grandma was going to wear on any given occasion. This same woman loved wearing her red hats to her Red Hat Society gatherings with her friends. (The Red Hat Society is based on a poem called "Warning" by British poet Jenny Joseph. The poem begins, "When I am an old woman I shall wear purple / With a red hat that doesn't go,...." The poem conveys the message that if you expect women "of a certain age" to dress or act in a certain way, think again.) Of course, this philosophy fit this Grandma well—her fancy red hat never went with the rest of her outfit. On the day of her funeral, her daughters and granddaughters all wore red hats to honor her. Imagine seeing a sea of red hats in a church at a funeral. What a perfect way to send Grandma off and remember her legacy.

Now imagine bringing this story to the granddaughter who loved her grandma dearly despite her choice of attire. This is wonderful evidence for the granddaughter but do you see how the evidence has gone beyond the physical description of the clothes? It brings in the story behind the clothes. It brings in the emotion. Such a story would be a "gold nugget" for this granddaughter.

My advice on physical descriptions is "Be mindful of stopping too soon. Dig a little deeper into the image. Uncover the hidden story." If you see something unusual in a clairvoyant image, use that in your descriptions. It's easy to fall into stereotypes, though, so be careful. Keep your logical mind at bay.

Stereotypes

As we learned from Nan, not all grandmothers have similar stories—many have extraordinary lives. One of our goals as a medium is to bring their story to life, allowing their loved ones here to relive those moments. It's like a celebration of their life.

In order for us to do this, we must move away from stereotypes and be open to whatever transpires. Here's a couple of stories that show how we need to "give what we get."

I was working in a church service one day and a gentleman came through for a family friend in the audience. The first piece of evidence was this incredible feeling of spinning out of control, falling rapidly, with a massive impact in the end. I knew that the impact had taken this gentleman's life. It felt as if it were a plane crash (but actually, it was a helicopter crash.) This was certainly not a typical way for someone to pass to the spirit world. The reading went on to show the lifestyle of this man—which again was not typical—he was into fast boats and trick water skiing. That's how he knew the woman in the audience.

One of the first readings I ever did for a stranger was of a little girl who came through to speak to her cousin. It was the first time this little girl had ever come through and her cousin was delighted. The first practical piece of evidence I received was about her passing. I felt a hard impact to her body and I saw a blue car. Of course, I immediately thought "car accident" but quickly got a "No" from the recipient. I knew there was a car involved and I knew this little girl had experienced blunt force trauma to her head. The recipient confirmed that was correct but it wasn't an accident. As this was my first attempt to give a reading, I didn't know what I was doing. I managed to go on and give evidence about the little girl. After the reading, the recipient told me that her cousin was pulled out of a car by her attacker. She died due to an impact to her head. She was just nine years old.

Once again, this was not stereotypical evidence, which shows that we as mediums must be open to receive what the spirit world needs to bring forward. Not all children die in car accidents or from an illness, and not all adults die from illnesses or heart attacks.

Clothing

As noted earlier, clothing can be very helpful in gathering unique evidence. Clothing reveals the time period in which the spirit communicator lived, which can be particularly helpful when discerning whether your communicator is a grandparent or a great-grandparent. Sometimes, for example, communicators show themselves in a uniform that specifies a time during a particular war. Clothing can also show a loved one's lifestyle, provide a bit of information about their personality, or display a specific memory. We can describe the clothing we see, but think of how much more valid describing the clothing is if we can delve into *why* a communicator is showing a particular piece of clothing. If all we do is describe what we see, we are leaving out important evidence to show who is with us. If we see ordinary clothing, we must ask ourselves, "Is it valuable evidence? Or is it vague evidence that most people could understand?" Always strive to give evidence that moves the story of the spirit communicator forward and makes them stand out in a crowd.

Never-ending Possibilities

Another seed for you to plant: When working with the spirit world, be open to never-ending possibilities. Step outside your comfort zone. Allow the spirit world to bring you unique evidence in many ways.

We can learn a lot from the story of Opa and Nan. Their story did not follow the norms of most grandparents; they were unique. I wonder, if we always dig deeper, what interesting stories will we uncover about the earthly lives of those who are now in the spirit world? We must strive to move beyond what we see clairvoyantly, knowing that many images hold a story that we don't understand immediately. But be careful— sometimes, images can be misleading!

Physical descriptions can be misleading too. Hairstyles, clothing, and body shapes change with time. For example, my mom and dad present themselves to mediums in their thirties, not at the age they passed or in the way they looked before they passed. Similarly, spirit communicators may present themselves with a full head of hair, but perhaps the recipient only remembers their loved one being bald. As you can see, there are times when physical descriptions or a style of clothing work—and times when they don't. So, use the information the spirit world presents in the most effective way. Be open to all the possibilities!

EXERCISE 1

Specific Evidence Part 1

Objective:

The aim of this exercise is to use only clairvoyant images and physical descriptions as evidence.

Type of Reading:

I recommend doing all of these readings as one-to-one sittings to get a good grasp on how to bring it all together. If you can get extra people or you are working in a circle, you may practice them in group or gallery settings. One-to-one settings are fifteen to thirty minutes long. Gallery style readings are seven to ten minutes long.

Materials Needed:

- Device to record your reading.
- Journal or notebook.
- Handout – Specific Evidence Images/Descriptions Only.
- Video – Using Specific Evidence Images/Descriptions Only.

Number of Participants:

- Two or more.

Table #8: Expectations: Specific Evidence – Part 1

Expectations: Specific Evidence	
Medium's Role	**Recipient's Role**
• Connect with the spirit world. • Only bring through evidence that physically describes the spirit communicator, e.g. hair, eyes, face, body, etc. • Delve deeper to uncover unusual physical aspects.	• The sitter is the time-keeper. Please let the medium know when they have exceeded their time. • Feedback should consist of "Yes," "No," "I don't know," or "I am not sure." • No additional feedback is necessary. • Record evidence on the handout.

Procedures:

1. Set your intent.
2. Hit "Record" on your phone or recorder.
3. Do the reading.
4. Stop recording.

Specific Evidence Part 2

Objective:

The aim of this exercise is to practice using specific types of evidence and to exclude clairvoyant images and physical descriptions.

Type of Reading:

I recommend doing all these readings as one-to-one sittings to get a good grasp on how to bring it all together. If you can get extra people or you are working in a circle, you may practice them in group or gallery settings. One-to-one sittings are fifteen to thirty minutes long. Gallery style readings are seven to ten minutes long.

Materials Needed:

- Device to record your reading.
- Journal or notebook.
- Specific Evidence Handout:
  All Clairs Except Clairvoyance.
- Specific Evidence Video (Optional): All Clairs Except Clairvoyance.

Number of Participants:

- Two or more.

Table #9: Expectations: Specific Evidence – Part 2

Expectations: Specific Evidence Part 2	
Medium's Role	**Recipient's Role**
• Connect with the spirit world. • Bring through evidence that excludes clairvoyant images and physically descriptions of the spirit communicator, i.e., NO evidence about hair, eyes, face, body, what they are wearing, etc. • Be open to using all your other clairs. • Evidence could include character traits, relationship, memories, work, family and friends, where they lived, and more.	• The sitter is the time-keeper. Please let the medium know when they have exceeded their time. • Feedback should consist of "Yes," "No," "I don't know," or "I am not sure." • No additional feedback is necessary.

Procedures:

1. Set your intent.
2. Hit "Record" on your phone or recorder.
3. Do the reading.
4. Stop recording.

Group Discussion:

- Compare and contrast the types of reading. Which parts felt different? Which parts were harder or easier?
- Were you able to identify the spirit communicator?
- Did any unusual information come forward?

- What was the "golden nugget," the bit you are the proudest you were able to do?
- What areas do you feel you need to work on in the future?
- What would you like to chat about with your guide or spirit helpers?

Journal:

- Reflect on how you feel about your reading today and write down your thoughts.
- Share any emotions or struggles that came up.
- What were your strengths? Where did you have challenges? Write these down.
- What was your "gold nugget," the best bit of the reading? Write it down.
- What seed did you plant today and how do you plan to nourish it in the future?
- Close your eyes. Take a few deep breaths. Ask your soul, "What wisdom do you want to leave with me today?" Wait for the answer to come—start writing.

Let us forget who we think we are,
so we may remember who we truly are, spirit.

The more we trust and surrender to the power within,
the less we try.

Chapter 6

"Surrendering"

Another Brick in the Wall

One day as our class was sitting in the lecture room at the Arthur Findlay College, our tutor gave us a task: Find a partner and give a reading. The lecture had covered several topics, but the main focus was expanding the evidence. This was a hot topic for me. I had spent months banging my head against a proverbial brick wall as I attempted to "expand my evidence." In fact, I was the one adding the bricks to that wall, making it even harder for myself.

This particular day was no different from all my other brick-wall days. I'd make a contact with the spirit world, bring them forward, give vague evidence, and then say, "Hello, Brick Wall." All week-long it had been *effort, wall, crash, repeat*. I refused to give up. "I will break through this wall" was my mantra. Being stubborn can come in handy at times!

The tutor had mentioned that when you hit a road block, you pause, turn, and take a drink of water. If you don't have a glass water, you take a drink in your mind. She assured us that the next piece of evidence would come, and the road block would disappear. I tried this during my readings. It helped a little but I still found it difficult to expand my evidence beyond vague evidence that anyone could have taken.

After what I deemed to be an utter failure of a reading, the tutor chose me as one of the mediums to demonstrate in the sanctuary that evening. I was shocked. "Is she crazy? Did she not just witness what happened in my reading?" I took a deep breath and nodded that I'd be happy to demonstrate. I only said "Yes" because I was too afraid to say "No." I fumbled through the rest of the day. Honestly, the only thing I could think of was standing on the sanctuary stage looking out at a sea of people. What gibberish would fall from my lips when I faced the audience?

After dinner, I went upstairs to my room to take a quick power nap. The days at the College are long and intense; you become exhausted emotionally and physically. I lay on the bed fighting the thoughts running through my head. I may have gotten five minutes of rest before the alarm on my phone reminded me it was time to get ready. I jumped in the shower in hopes of reviving myself. I changed my clothes, then headed downstairs to join the other mediums in the large lounge to prepare for the evening. The tutor came in ... Did we have the order of mediums decided? She gave us a pep talk and reminded us to take a drink of water if we hit a roadblock.

We made our way to the sanctuary, found our seats on stage, and watched as the seats in the house began to fill. My nerves were through the roof. I remember the tutor saying earlier in the day, "Use your nerves to your advantage." I wasn't sure what that meant or how to do it but I was trying with all my might to make it happen.

It was time to begin. The chairperson introduced the mediums for the night and gave the audience instructions. I was second on the list. The first medium stood to begin. I closed my eyes and prayed—prayed I'd be able to stand up when my name was called, prayed I could speak, prayed for my guide to come, prayed I'd make a contact.

The first medium finished. The audience clapped. Somewhere amid the droning of hands I heard, "...Kay Reynolds." My stomach churned. A knot formed in my throat. I took a deep breath, stood up, and said to my spirit team, "We're up, let's rock and roll." I remembered that there are two things that ease my nerves: smiling and cracking a joke. I made my way to the front of the stage, peered out at the audience, smiled, and told a joke. The audience laughed—success! I'd raised the vibration in the room. I closed my eyes for a second to take my focus to the spirit world. I became aware of a woman from the spirit world, a mother. As I began to work with her, I realized she was not the nicest of moms. In fact, she was a difficult person to be around and her relationship with her son was scary at best. I had not yet learned how to find my recipient, so I threw this information out to the audience. Two gentlemen raised their hands. They were sitting one in front of the other; both were American. I went back and forth between the two gentlemen before finally halfway deciding I was with the one sitting in the front. I continued giving evidence. The gentleman in the back was nodding his head, "Yes," along with the one in the front. I hadn't found the correct sitter. I took a drink of water, stepped back into my power, and turned around. The evidence didn't come. I mumbled a few more pieces of vague evidence, took another drink, moved back into my power. I turned and said, "This mother was not native to America." The gentleman in front nodded "Yes," the one in the back shook his head "No." Yes! Finally, a little success. I continued on, then bang ... I hit another wall. I took another drink.

Nothing. I repeated a few strong "Yes's" to give my ego a boost, took another drink ... and hit the brick wall. This went on for some time. I looked toward the back of the room where my tutor was busy writing down everything I said and did. She never looked up ... I was on my own.

I did the only thing I knew to do. I pointed out the highlights to end on a positive note and thanked the gentleman for working with me. I made my next contact which went better and exited to the back of the stage as quickly as I could, feeling a bit defeated by the first reading.

As I sat on the stage waiting for the other mediums to finish, I couldn't help but wonder, "How much water must a medium drink to help expand the evidence?" I'd taken a lot of sips of water and it only worked a few times. "Man, if only I could change the water to wine I'm sure I'd do much better!" It was a nice thought but we all know there can only be one kind of 'spirit' helping us while we work. Ahh, what am I doing wrong?

My tutor had said I needed to surrender and trust the spirit world to lead the story being unfolded. At the time, I didn't know what that meant. For the next few years, I heard "Surrender and trust" every time I hit that wall. I thought I was already surrendering and trusting. Before every reading, I would say a prayer, surrender to God, and put my trust in Him and in the spirit world. The problem was, they were only words. On the inside, I didn't believe it. I didn't fully understand what those words meant ... so how could I believe in it from the inside?

How to Surrender?

I learned later in my training the true meaning of "surrendering." It's far more than saying the words, that's for sure. It's more about the medium letting go of control and being active in the reading, but being passive at the same time. It sounds crazy I know. It's about trusting that the spirit communicator knows more about their needs and the recipient's needs than the medium does—and the medium stepping back, passive, allowing the communicator to take the lead. The medium is silently (without knowing it) conveying this message to their communicator, "I trust you, you know exactly where we need to go. Show me the way. I'm here to be your voice. I surrender to your needs."

Control versus Surrender

When we think of surrendering, we must look at the opposite of surrender, which is control. Controlling our readings or contacts is one of the biggest causes of hitting those brick walls I talked about. I was controlling the reading and it was not going well—for me, the communicator, or for the recipient.

Control = Brick Wall – Stalls – Crash and Burn – Resistance .

Surrender = Flow – Ease – Feels Right.

What does that look like when we are in the midst of a reading? Take a look at the diagram on Control versus Surrender.

Table #10: Control/Surrender

Control	Surrender
• Demands specific types of evidence, i.e., checklists.	• Passive enough to allow spirit to take the lead.
• Who knows more about the needs of the recipient, spirit or the medium?	• You feel with the center of being, your solar plexus.
• Demands how the evidence images are given - interferes with naturalness.	• Communication flows – no resistance.
• Deciding what is the good evidence and what isn't ... i.e., too vague, too unusual.	
• Asking questions – takes you into your head – moves awareness out of the power	
• Lack of open and honest relationship with self	

Demands

As I mentioned earlier, many mediumship tutors give their students a list of criteria to help them learn to "structure" their readings: Get the spirit communicator's age, their manner of passing, a physical description, and so forth. Such lists are great in the beginning to help new mediums see what types of evidence can come through. It's a useful strategy but students don't always approach it in the most productive way. We have to find a balance: actively building structure while passively allowing our spirit communicator to lead us on a journey. If we pursue structure and control at the expense of flow, we limit the spirit communicator and dictate to the spirit world what we want from them. Remember, as mediums we are in service to the spirit world— not the other way around.

The same is true when you are working from a list. Many tutors teach, "Use the List." But when you have "the List" in your head, you keep going back to the List instead of staying with your spirit communicator. When that happens, you drop out of your power—you are no longer with your spirit communicator—you are in your own mind.

As you can see, structure and lists are tricky. It's like walking a tightrope: Balance is key. Go too far, you may find yourself in a quandary. So, let the structural details float in your head, hold on to your list of possibilities, but be flexible. Don't forget, your spirit communicator knows which direction to go and which evidence they want you to bring through. Trust your communicator, move with them, and don't place demands.

Many mediums not only mandate that their spirit communicator deliver the items on the List, but also require that the evidence comes through in a certain way: We petition the spirit world for "images only," or we want to open our ear chakras and *hear* the evidence. I've even seen mediums require evidence to come in a set order. *Oh my.* Imagine what the spirit world is thinking when we place such high demands: "What *is* this woman doing?"

I recently went to a new doctor. On my first visit, she asked me to tell her anything I felt she needed to know about me. As I went on about my ailments and past medical history, she didn't interrupt, didn't demand to know about things I didn't share. She trusted me to give her all the information she'd need to meet my needs. I felt validated, knowing she wanted me to take the lead in my health care. Of course, she allowed her expertise to come in when it was needed but she was passive when I needed her to be and active when her expertise was required. In a similar way, we as mediums have to learn when to be passive (allowing spirit to lead us) and when to become active (allowing our soul to rise and lead the way).

It is true that in workshops or training, we give the spirit world our agenda, so we can learn new techniques. I believe our guides and spirit helpers are happy to be flexible and accommodate us in these learning situations—after all, they are our teachers. That said, we still must be passive and allow them to lead us as they teach us.

Decision-Making

Raise your hand if you have disregarded evidence because you didn't trust it. I raise my hand high on this one—I'm the queen of deciding if the evidence was "good enough" or "too-good-to-believe." I've passed up really good evidence because I didn't believe it was coming from the communicator. For example, I was doing a demonstration in London one night and the first bit of evidence I received was that my communicator, the uncle of my recipient, was a millionaire. I dismissed it, thinking, "No way. It must be my imagination." So right off the bat, I sent the message to my communicator: "I don't trust you." Not good. Fortunately, he stayed with me anyway and I gave a decent reading. Afterward, the recipient told me his uncle was a self-made millionaire. *Ouch.* My lesson that night (and on many nights to follow) was to trust in my communicator, to never decide what's "good evidence" or "too-good-to-be-true" evidence, and to be confident and give evidence as I receive it. This was a huge lesson for me, and believe me, it did not happen overnight.

Questions

If you are like me, you learned early on to ask your spirit communicator questions. This is another tricky one. As I mentioned before, the problem I had (and likely one you will have as well) was that I went into my head for the questions. As we know, thinking is the best way to take us out of our power, away from the communicator—and straight into that wall we all love to hit. Over the years, I learned that there's an art to asking questions. You cry out to the spirit world from the core of your being, from your soul, from your spirit. This way, you remain in your power because in this type of petition, your soul, not your head, is communicating with the spirit world. The other key point is to leave your questions open-ended, leaving the decision about what to share up to the communicator. Two questions I use are:

1. Is there anything else you'd like to say? and
2. Your loved one doesn't understand, is there another way to say it?

This allows the spirit communicator to be in control and keeps the medium from asking specific questions or placing demands.

Surrender

Surrendering during a reading is letting go of control, it's a fine balance between being passive enough to allow the spirit communicator to work with you to meet their needs and knowing when to be active. To surrender, you trust the spirit world completely, step out of the way, and become a voice for the voiceless. You'll know you've learned the art of surrendering once it all begins to work smoothly. Your readings will flow, you'll allow the communicator to lead the way, and you'll know when to step in and be more active. It will feel wonderful!

Letting Go

It's human nature to want to control the situations we find ourselves in. No matter the subject, letting go is always hard. Think of a time in your life when you knew you needed to let go but found it difficult. Yet once you did it, it was as if the universe was conspiring with you to make sure all was well in your world. It's that way in mediumship. It's hard to "Let go and let spirit." Yet, when we do, everything clicks. Your readings flow. New doors open for you in your work with the spirit world.

Surrendering is like trusting. When I first sat with my guide all those years ago, what I believe he was conveying to me was to trust in the information I received and to trust the spirit world to deliver the evidence that needed to be heard. I received the same message as I sat with him daily in meditation for many months afterward. I would ask him, "How can I be a better medium?" His answer was "Trust." It frustrated me, that's for sure. I didn't understand it at the time but now I get it totally.

Remember that acorn I planted? For me, the journey to learning how to surrender followed the growth pattern of the oak tree. I planted the acorn, I nurtured it as often as I could, I fed and watered it. I watched it grow from a tiny sapling to a mighty oak. It grew strong roots and it swayed in the wind in perfect balance—just enough sway to move with the wind yet strong enough to not break. It was beautiful to behold. I was proud of the work I'd done.

Nurturing that seed wasn't easy. I had to trust myself. To trust myself, I had to believe in myself. To believe in myself, I had to know myself. To know myself, I needed to know my spirit—that one aspect of me that carries the spark of the Creator. From there I began to heal from the inside out.

Once I learned to trust in me, the next step was to trust in the spirit world. This took time. I like being in control. In my teaching career, I taught little people. With twenty-five little souls confined to one room all day long, I had to be in complete control—it was ingrained in my being. I had to relearn how to let go. It was liberating to allow someone else to take the lead and once I had the taste of that sweet freedom, it felt good. It felt right.

The excitement I felt on a soul level was electrifying. You see, for the first time in my fifty-something years, my soul was free to fly and do what it came here to do. So, I say to you: "Work on you, trust in yourself and in spirit, let go ... and allow your soul to fly. Once you do, communicating with your spirit communicators will flow with ease."

Blending with Spirit Meditation

Objective:

The aim of this exercise is to learn how to blend with the spirit world on a deeper level, to help you move your evidence to a deeper level.

Materials Needed:

- Device to guide you in the meditation.
- Meditation Recording – Create your own meditation recording or go to my website to listen to mine.

Number of Participants:

- One or more.

Table #11: Expectations: Blending with Spirit Meditation

Expectations: Blending with Spirit Meditation	
Medium's Role	Recipient's Role
• Use this meditation once a week in place of sitting in your power.	• Not applicable

Procedures:

1. Relax.
2. Follow the guided meditation.
3. Stop recording.

Meditation

Blending with Spirit

You have two choices with the meditation:

1. You can use the meditation below to create your own recording of a meditation to follow.
2. You can go to my website to listen to the recording I've done to guide you through the meditation.

We are all spiritual beings housed in a physical body, placed here on this earth temporarily for different reasons. If you believe that we are all connected, then surely you can understand how simple it is for our spirit within to reconnect with the unseen world; how easy it is for us to connect with the Creator of all and to be in touch with our own spirit. Imagine the possibility of a oneness of all things, in both this world and the unseen world. Through this oneness, we are able to connect with all spiritual beings, all things the creator placed here on Earth.

This meditation is designed for you to connect with a spirit communicator—it can be a guide or a loved one. It does not matter who the spirit communicator is; the aim is to blend your energy with their energy. When we work with the spirit world, we can strengthen our connection with the spirit communicator by allowing them to come very close to us, blending their energy with ours. This exercise teaches you how to do this. This is not a deep trance state. It is simply a deeper connection when channeling spirit. (Please note: Pregnant women and those with health concerns should check with their doctors before doing this exercise.)

Find a nice comfortable place in a room or outside. Make sure you are warm and have no distractions. Begin by closing your eyes and breathing naturally, allowing the tension to release from your body.

Now, take three deep, cleansing breaths on the count of 4. Deep breath in ... 1 2 3 4 ... hold 1 2 3 4 ... and release 1 2 3 4. Again, deep breath in ... 1 2 3 4 ... hold 1 2 3 4 ... and release 1 2 3 4 ... And one more time ... Deep breath in ... 1 2 3 4 ... hold 1 2 3 4 ... and release 1 2 3 4. Return to normal breathing.

Allow all thoughts to move past you. Breathe and be in this present moment.

Imagine a beautiful light descending from above you. You know this is the light of your creator, all loving, all knowing.

Breathe this light into your body. Allow it to fill every cell. Be in this moment with your creator.

From the soul of your being, invite a spirit communicator of your choice to come and be with you. Ask them to stand closer than they've ever stood before. Now, ask them to place their hands upon your hands, allowing the energy to blend in a way that you become aware of the characteristics of your communicator's hands.

Ask your communicator to place their feet upon your feet. Allow their feet to blend in such a way that their feet become your feet. What do you notice?

Breathing into this stillness, ask your communicator to blend completely with you, allowing their thoughts to become your thoughts. Sit with your communicator, allowing the full blending as long as it feels comfortable for you. Feel the love that emanates from you and your communicator. This is your time to sit in the presence of spirit.

Before we bring this to a close, share any last thoughts with your communicator and give thanks to the communicator for coming to be with you.

Your time with your communicator is coming to a close.

Feel the love that emanates from you and from your communicator.

Ask your communicator what it wishes you to know. Pay attention to thoughts, visions, words, or feelings that come at this time.

Give thanks to your communicator and say your goodbyes.

Breathing into the stillness, make your way back to the room in which you sit.

Wiggle your toes, take a deep breath, and stretch.

Namaste.

Let Go and Let Spirit

This simple meditation helps you to let go and let spirit take the lead. It prepares you to blend beautifully and seamlessly with your sitter's loved ones in the spirit world. Remember, the deeper the blending of spirit, the deeper your evidence will be. Your sitter and the spirit world will be grateful you learned to blend deeper. I think you will be too!

I have a guided meditation on my website of this exercise. I recommend you do this meditation exercise once a week. It will help you in many ways.

Journal:

- Reflect on how you feel about your meditation today. Write down your thoughts.
- Share any emotions or struggles that may have come up.
- What did you feel were your strengths? What was challenging?
- What did you become aware of about the communicator?
- Close your eyes, take a few deep breaths, and ask your soul what wisdom it wants to leave with you today. Wait for it to come. Start writing.

There's always room for a story that can transport people to another place.

—J.K. Rowling

CHAPTER 7

"WEAVING THE STORY"

Mediums are the bridge between two worlds—the spirit world and the physical world. If we truly surrender to the spirit world, our communicators will weave a story for us to share with our recipient. That story can transport a grieving sitter to a place filled with loving memories—how wonderful it is for the spirits of loved ones in both worlds when they walk away feeling joy and peace within!

In Chapter 2, I mentioned that on the first day of my mentorship with Mavis Pittilla, I had done a "mind journey." It was the first time I had heard that terminology. For me, it was like a watching a movie; the images were 3-D, with vivid colors flying through my mind's eye. I called them "movies in my head" prior to hearing Mavis call them "mind journeys." I know now that it is the spirit communicator who takes the medium on the journey, giving us a wonderful opportunity to weave a story and access a whole new realm of spirit world interaction.

What are Mind Journeys and Why Are They Important?

As noted, when spirit communicators use images to bring their story alive, scenes of the spirit person's life roll effortlessly through your mind, almost like you are watching a movie in full technicolor action. Mind journeys can enhance your mediumship in several ways. First, you have to surrender to the spirit communicator and let them take the lead. There's no time to stop and ponder the evidence or reflect on "the List." You have to give your recipient the information that's coming through quickly because there is a continuous flow—each piece of evidence arrives just as you share the piece before it—and the communicator's story unfolds naturally.

While mind journeys use primarily your clairvoyance, they can bring in other clairs too. For example, you may suddenly pick up on smells (like smelling the musty odor of an attic) or be able to taste (like tasting the salt in the sea air near the loved one's home). Or, you might feel the emotions connected to the scene that is unfolding in your mind's eye. This is what is so beautiful about mind journeys—once you surrender, spirit will bring you evidence in multiple ways.

In life, I am a private person, there is not a nosy bone in me. I keep to myself and don't pry into other people's business. When doing mind journeys, however, we have permission to be nosy. This is hard for me. I had to ease into this nosy bit—but hey, it's kind of fun, once you get past your own issues.

When a spirit communicator takes you into their house and you see furniture or cupboards with drawers or doors, peek inside. You can learn a lot about a person when you see what is hidden in their drawers. Perhaps they have led you to the second drawer in the nightstand because there is a special memory there that was left for a family member. Or perhaps they'll take you to a dresser where a certain book always sat, and guide you to specific page in that book (that now belongs to their daughter) because it has a beautiful message for her that she needs to hear today.

I've learned through the years that there's always a reason for a mind journey. Your communicators take you to the areas they lived in to show you the kind of life they once had, and to show you memories they hold dear. They take you into their homes to bring special memories to life. You will often find gold nuggets within the evidence on a mind journey and it's up to you, the medium, to allow the important elements of every mind journey to unfold.

Mind Journey in East Los Angeles

I gave a reading to a young man whose brother had not been in the spirit world long. I knew a little about the recipient; he was once a concert pianist who had been well on his way to becoming famous. Word spread quickly and the demands of the Hollywood producers became overwhelming. In the end, he chose to live a quieter life, teaching piano in another country far away from Hollywood.

I was happy to give this young man a reading. A man came through right away. As usual, the communicator's personality came through first. He had a soft side but he also had a toughness about him and a wall built around him. The next bit of evidence I received was an image of this man working on a car parked in the road. I knew this man loved his car and liked to tinker around with the engine even if he wasn't really fixing anything. I could see grease under his fingernails. As I watched him working, I could hear yelling coming from the house and he kept looking back at the house.

The next thing I knew he took me inside the house. I could see children running around. As he took me through the house, I became aware of the emotions—anger, confusion, and blame coming from those who lived there. I could see a woman yelling at this gentleman. Next, he took me back outside into the neighborhood. I felt immediately as if I would never walk alone in this neighborhood, it wasn't safe. The houses were all similar. He took me down the road and he showed me an intersection. On one corner of the intersection was a convenience store. He shared childhood memories of himself and his siblings buying cigarettes at the convenience store. I knew we were in a big city and the convenience store wasn't a place for a child to be on their own. I knew illegal activities took place there. This gave me insight into the life of this gentleman in his younger years. As we made our way down the street, I could see his life unfolding. Childhood was difficult at best. He showed me the tough exterior that surrounded him and that he wasn't always a pleasant guy.

At the end of the reading, I learned he was the sitter's brother. He wanted to go down memory lane to remind his brother of life as they knew it but, more importantly, he wanted his brother to know he wasn't always the tough guy. He felt he had to be tough to survive. Just before he said goodbye, he moved beyond the tough exterior and let his brother know how much he cared for him. It was exactly what his brother needed to hear. My sitter was delighted, the spirit communicator was happy, and I must admit I was proud of my work that day.

I had experienced mind journeys before but this one was different. This mind journey moved beyond clairvoyant images and allowed my other clairs to shine. I could feel the energy and emotions that matched each scene. I felt as if I were really there. This was new and so exciting for me. I felt as if I'd made a major shift in my development that day. I couldn't wait to do another mind journey!

You Can Do This

I know developing mediumship can become overwhelming at times. Trust me when I say: If I can learn to do this, you can too! The reading I just shared took place in the early years of my development. It was not perfect. I had a few wobbles: I paused when I should have trusted, I uttered "Ummm" too often before speaking (which was a stall tactic), and I didn't get the relationship of the man until the end. But the mind journey was amazing. I could have beaten myself up for all the wobbles but I decided to celebrate what came together instead. I was a beginner. I made notes of what to work on and did a happy dance for stepping out of the way and trusting the spirit communicator to lead the way.

Just as I make no demands on the evidence I want from the spirit world, I don't try to force mind journeys. I allow the evidence to flow freely as the spirit communicator chooses. But if I become aware of the communicator wanting to take me on a journey, I run with it because I know there will be opportunities for great evidence and shared memories—and possibly even a gold nugget for my sitter.

Here are a few key points to remember about mind journeys:

1. Mind journeys are images used to bring the communicator's story to life.
2. Images roll quickly through your mind like a movie.
3. With the images, you may become aware of sounds, smells, tastes, or emotions.
4. As one piece of evidence rolls from your lips, another piece has arrived, waiting for you to give it to your sitter.
5. You must leave "the List" of specific evidence behind to allow the communicator to bring to you what they wish.

Mind journeys don't have to happen every time you give a reading. There are no rules. It all depends on you the medium and your spirit communicator. Spirit will bring through evidence in the way it works for both of you. The important thing is to open up to new ways of working. It's always better to offer the spirit world many choices on ways to work with you instead of only one or two options. So, give yourself time to allow this aspect of your mediumship to unfold.

Remember, today's mighty oak is yesterday's nut that held its ground!

Weaving a Story

Storytelling is in my genes. I grew up listening to family members tell stories about our ancestors. I taught my little students in the classroom through story, so allowing spirit world stories to unfold was a natural process for me. I can't think of a better way to honor those in the spirit world than to share a snippet of their life story with the recipient. But even though it is natural for me to tell stories, because I am a teacher, in my early development, I still struggled with letting go of control. I mean, honestly, I wanted to have complete lesson plans written out for every reading I did. If only it were that simple!

Letting go of control is challenging. I worked on it for several years. Listening to my recordings helped me realize that in order to maintain control in my readings, I was holding on to information. During a reading, I was unaware I was doing it but when I listened back, it was obvious. Having a tutor point out when I was holding back helped too. The more I became aware of how I was controlling my readings, the more I began to "let go and let spirit."

Oma

I was giving a reading to a woman one day and became aware of her Oma ("grandmother" in German). I began the reading as I normally do, bringing through typical evidence of an Oma. As I was giving the evidence, I could sense my recipient wasn't too impressed, she was expecting far more than I was giving her. I had a moment of panic, took a deep breath, and cried out to the spirit world. A scene began to unfold in front of me. I could see lots of children everywhere in what felt like a home. My mind immediately came into the picture. I thought, "I must have an Oma here who took care of many children, most likely grandchildren and children from around the neighborhood." The recipient understood the children but not in the way I thought. I took another breath and continued. I became aware of these children not being blood-related to Oma. The recipient nodded. The more I worked with this Oma, the more her story moved away from my own logical thinking. I had an internal struggle going on between what I felt and what I thought. I knew I was in another country, a country in which people did not speak English. I also knew there was sadness surrounding these children. It was the sadness that felt odd. I couldn't put my finger on what I was feeling. I hadn't ever felt this in a reading before, so I was reluctant to share it with the recipient. I held on to it.

I continued on with the reading and when I brought it to an end, the recipient and I began chatting about her Oma. I explained the sadness with the children and that I couldn't quite put my finger on why they were so sad. She explained that her Oma worked in a home, in Belgium, which cared for orphans separated from their parents during the Holocaust. I was disappointed—I had missed this crucial part of her Oma's life story.

Blending Soul-to-Soul

Earlier, we discussed the importance of surrendering. When you surrender, you allow the spirit world to come close and allow a blending of souls: your soul with the soul of the spirit communicator. When I brought this Oma through, I had not yet learned to surrender or how to blend soul-to-soul, to allow the spirit communicator to tell their story. I still wanted control. I knew I had to learn to blend deeper; I had a lot of work ahead of me. I wanted to step out of the way and allow the spirit communicators to tell their story.

Working on Blending

Sitting in the power and sitting with your guide will help you learn to blend and surrender to the spirit world. Once you've learned to surrender fully, the blending takes place naturally. In my own development, I would sit with the spirit world and practice blending. I would ask them to come closer and closer. I wanted their thoughts to become my thoughts, their hands to become my hands. I wanted to blend so fully that I felt as if I were them, I wanted to mimic their facial expressions or the way their body moved in a certain way.

Through years of practice this became a part of me. When I stepped into my power to work, the blending of souls occurred naturally. I no longer had to ask spirit to come closer and closer. That blending was already established with me, my spirit team, and the communicator. This is where we want our development to be in order to allow spirit to tell their story.

The Structure of a Story

There is a structure to unfolding a story of a spirit communicator's life. It is not a list of "must haves," so please don't see it in this way. We must be flexible in our readings. As a teacher in the classroom, I had lesson plans to guide me each day, but as a professional educator, I was flexible and knew that things might not go in the order I had planned or unfold exactly as I had hoped. Giving a reading is the same.

First, I set my intent to allow spirit to lead me. My spirit team is aware of my intent. They convey my intent to my spirit communicator. The spirit world collaborates on what they hope to carry out. Once a reading begins, the plan from spirit is set into motion. Then it is up to the medium and the spirit communicator to do their best to make it happen, moving with the flow and unfolding the story.

My hope is to bring forward the types of evidence that will tell the story of the communicator. I trust the communicator to share events or life stories that the recipient will understand. As mediums, we use our words to heal. My hope always is to heal in this world and in the unseen world. I want to touch the souls of all who are listening or involved in some way.

Establishing who my communicator is (in a private sitting and in a platform reading) and who my recipient is (if I'm doing a demonstration) are the first two things I want to accomplish quickly. The rest can go in any order. It's up to my communicator to lead the way. Weaving a story may have some of these characteristics or types of evidence:
- Establish the identity of the communicator.
- Balance the reading with the essence of the communicator and practical evidence or memories.

- Go on a mind journey or two.
- Share memories, hobbies, work, accomplishments, what brought them joy, or anything the communicator feels is important.
- Share with your sitter or recipient whom the communicator has reunited with in the spirit world, and how they spend their time in the spirit world.
- Create a story that brings the communicator to life, so the recipient can feel their essence.
- Create a story that captivates audience members too.
- Find The Wow Factor—the gold nugget that takes the breath of the recipient or audience away.

Use this list as a guide only. If your readings go in a different direction, that's okay. Sometimes the best readings happen when you go off course.

Wrong Place, Wrong Time

The unfolding of a communicator's story reminds me of a reading I did while working with an online spirit art practice group. I set my intent to connect with a loved one in the spirit world who belonged to a member of the group. A young man from the spirit world (I'll call him Jack), in his later teens or early twenties, came to me. I am not a spirit artist but I enjoy working in this way from time to time. As I was drawing, I worked with him. Facial features began to form and evidence of his character began to flow. Once I was finished drawing, I put my focus on gathering more evidence.

I knew right away that Jack had come to speak to his mother, who was connected to the practice group. I knew Jack had a lot of energy about him, was always on the go, couldn't sit still, and that sometimes this would get him into trouble. I knew he was not always the best student at school. He struggled with his lessons and it was not easy for him to focus. I knew he came from a home that struggled with finances. His family was hard-working but barely made enough money to get by at the end of the month. Sometimes, they would need help from the government. As I got confirmation from his mother, my confidence grew and the communication with Jack began to take off.

I became aware of Jack passing suddenly. My mind jumped in and assumed he was in a car wreck but I realized that wasn't the case. I had a strong feeling of his life being cut short at the hands of another person. The more I worked with him, the more I felt as if he'd been murdered.

His mother confirmed I was right. As soon as I got the confirmation, I felt Jack taking me to the scene of the murder. As I mentioned in the last chapter, I felt as if I was *there*. I knew it was after midnight. I could feel cold, damp air and I knew the area was not the safest place to be at night. I could see Jack walking and coming upon an argument between a group of people. By the time he reached the group, the argument had escalated into a fist fight. Jack stepped in to try to de-escalate the situation. His efforts were not received well, and the group turned on him and began to beat him. He was murdered right there.

His mother confirmed everything.

From here, my mind journey was over and it was up to me to tell the rest of Jack's story. He made me aware of a court trial of three boys. All three were acquitted. He also made me aware of a young woman who'd been a witness but she had refused to come forward. The mother confirmed the three were acquitted and she said the family had always believed there was a witness who wasn't coming forward. They also believed it was a woman. The reading closed with Jack giving a message. He wanted his mother to tell his brother to stop blaming himself for the murder. His brother had felt he did not do enough to stop Jack from going to that part of town. It turned out that the picture I had drawn was not of Jack. It was a picture of Jack's brother who was carrying the blame. Jack wanted his brother to let it go, he wanted him to know that there was nothing he could have said or done to keep him from going out that night.

Reflection on this Reading

When I reflect on this reading, I realize how important it was for me to let go of control and let spirit lead the way. The spirit communicator came forward at the start, he shared his personality, his age, and told me whom he wanted to speak to. He set the scenes up for the story to show itself naturally. He took me on a mind journey to allow the beginnings of the story to unfold and from there, made me aware of key pieces of evidence in regard to his passing. There were two important messages hidden in the story:

- His family needed to hear that there had been a witness who had chosen not to come forward. They needed this confirmation and to know they were on the right track in their search.
- The spirit communicator needed to tell his little brother to stop blaming himself for the murder. There was nothing he could have said or done differently to change the communicator's mind about going to that area of town. It wasn't his brother's fault.

There were holes in the story I delivered. I wish I could have brought forward the name of the witness. I wish I had known that the picture I drew was of the living brother, not the communicator. The reading itself was choppy. I had to work hard to bring evidence through, so, while the evidence was good, if you were listening to my delivery, you might have tilted your head to one side and raised your eyebrows.

I was impressed at how well the spirit communicator did at letting the story unfold. He brought in all the key elements to get his point across so that healing could begin with his family. Overall, I was happy with the outcome because the important messages for this boy's mom and brother were loud and clear.

Stepping Stones

Mind journeys are a stepping stone in the unfolding of a spirit communicator's story. They provide opportunities for us as mediums to get out of our heads and allow spirit to lead. So, as I said earlier, when a loved one in spirit takes you into their home, be nosy. Open cupboards and drawers. Examine the keepsakes closely. Turn the tea cup over, look for the emblem on the bottom. Why is that tea cup important enough that spirit wanted to show it to you? Mind journeys are a great way to learn all about your communicator.

Learning to unfold the story in a reading is one of my fondest memories of my training. I believe it was what my soul was yearning for me to do from the beginning. It felt good. It felt right—and, more importantly, I saw a difference in my client's reactions to the readings. I know the spirit world was happier because finally it was their story being told, in the way they chose.

It took a few years of practice to get to where I wanted to be, which forced me to dig deep to find the patience and the perseverance to keep going. As I've noted, the biggest hurdle was letting go and letting spirit. So, remember, there is no magic pill to help you to let go. It's all about doing the inner work. I've heard so many times: "Work on yourself, Kay." I learned that if you have trust issues when giving a reading, it's a direct result of what's happening to you on the inside. So, off I'd go, to sit alone in quiet contemplation—and sometimes, sit with my guide in silence. I never really knew what took place during those times but I do know a flood of emotions would come bubbling up to the surface. Some days, I'd come out of meditation with tears rolling down my cheeks.

The rest of the work I did to help me learn to unfold the story and get to the Wow factor was practice, practice, and more practice. As you practice, work toward narrowing down the evidence to key pieces, because those pieces are loaded with more information. Be open to all types of evidence and don't forget, you can always dig a little deeper to find hidden evidence behind the evidence you have received. Enjoy the process, celebrate each step along the way, and know: *If I can do it, so can you.* Each time you delve a little deeper and weave the story of your spirit communicator's life, you are nurturing the seeds you've planted. When storytelling comes to fruition, your acorn is maturing, and your oak tree is standing strong and tall.

EXERCISE 1

Mind Journey

Objective:

The aim is to let go and surrender to spirit, allowing the spirit communicator to take you on a mind journey.

Type of Reading:

I recommend doing all these readings as one-to-one sittings to get a good grasp on how to bring it all together. You may practice them in group or gallery settings if you can get extra people or are working in a circle. One-to-one sittings are fifteen to thirty minutes long. Gallery style readings are seven to ten minutes long.

Materials Needed:

- Device to record your reading.
- Journal or Notebook.
- Video – Mind Journey (Optional).

Number of Participants:

- Two or more.

Table #12: Expectations: Mind Journey

Expectations: Mind Journey	
Medium's Role	**Recipient's Role**

• Connect with the spirit world.
 	
• Begin your reading.
 	
• Relax and let the communicator take you on a journey.
 	
• Give main piece of evidence, then add three or four more pieces of evidence that tie into the main evidence.
 	
• Here are some things you may become aware of during the reading:
 	
   • Was the furniture worn? Was it old or new?
 	
   • How is the furniture placed in the room?
 	
   • Are there doors or windows in the room?
 	
   • What did they do while in a particular room? Watch TV? Knit? Play with a pet?
 	
   • What objects can you see? Is there a favorite picture?
 	
   • Is the house tidy or cluttered? Bright or dark?
 	
   • What memories are held in this room?
 	
   • Are you aware of emotions?
	• The sitter is the time-keeper. Please let the medium know when they've exceeded their time.
	
	• Feedback should consist of "Yes," "No," "I don't know," or "I'm not sure."
	
	• No additional feedback is necessary.
	
	• Sitter takes notes of evidence using handout.

Procedures:

1. Set your intent.
2. Hit "Record" on your phone or recorder.
3. Do the reading.
4. Stop recording.

Discussion with Group or Partner About the Process or Exercise:
- What stood out as your strengths?
- Which was easier to do, psychic or mediumship? Explain your thinking.
- What areas will you place your focus on for the next time you practice these exercises?
- Looking ahead, what is your plan to bring mind journeys forward as an option for your clients in the spirit world?
- Will you continue to practice?
- What kind of chat will you have with your spirit team about how they can help you?

Journal:

- Reflect on how you feel about your reading today. Write down your thoughts.
- Share any emotions or struggles that may have come up.
- What were your strengths? Where did you have challenges?
- What was your gold nugget, the best bit of the reading?
- Close your eyes, take a few deep breaths, and ask your soul what wisdom it wants to leave with you today. Wait for it to come. Start writing.

Narrowing the Evidence

Objective:

The aim of this exercises is to narrow your evidence to key pieces, expand on the key pieces of evidence, and allow the story to unfold.

Type of Reading:

I recommend doing all these readings as one-to-one sittings to get a good grasp on how to bring it all together. You may practice them in group or gallery settings if you can get extra people or are working in a circle. For the purpose of this exercise, one-to-one sittings are fifteen to thirty minutes long. Gallery style readings are seven to ten minutes long.

Materials Needed:

- Device to record your reading.
- Journal or Notebook.
- Handout – Narrowing the Evidence.
- Video – Narrowing the Evidence (Optional).

Number of Participants:

- Two or more.

Table #13: Expectations: Narrowing the Evidence

Expectations: Narrowing the Evidence	
Medium's Role	**Recipient's Role**
• Connect with the spirit world.	• The sitter is the time-keeper. Please let the medium know when they've exceeded their time.
• Hold your power for the length of the reading.	
• Bring evidence through.	• Give answers of "Yes," "No," or "I don't know," with no other feedback.
• Choose one or two pieces you feel will have more hidden information.	• If the medium gives a piece of evidence that you know has a lot of information hidden inside, give the medium a nudge by telling them to stay with that piece of evidence.
• Blend your energy or move into the energy of the evidence to see what else is revealed.	
• If the recipient tells you to stay with a piece of evidence, stay with it to see what else is there.	

Procedures:

1. Set your intent.
2. Hit "Record" on your phone or recorder.
3. Do the reading.
4. Stop recording.

Handout:

Table #14: Narrowing the Evidence – Sitter Records the Evidence in the Appropriate Column

Narrowing the Evidence Sitter records the evidence in the appropriate column.			
General (Character Traits/ relationship/ emotion)	General (Physical Descriptions/ clothing)	Strong (Memory)	Strong (Work/hobby/ mind journey)

We want to spend the majority of our time with strong evidence. This is where we find the gold nuggets. Circle the strong evidence you'd like the medium to spend more time on for more evidence. Example of what this exercise may look like:

Table #15: Narrowing the Evidence

Narrowing the Evidence Example			
General (Character Traits/ relationship/ emotion)	**General (Physical Descriptions/ clothing)**	**Strong (Memory)**	**Strong (Work/ hobby/mind journey)**
• Man • Father • Kind • Family man	• Tall • Dark hair • Average build • Tan pants • Plaid shirt • Baseball hat	• Camping in Yosemite • Skiing in Jackson Hole • Backyard BBQ's *Digging deeper into Camping in Yosemite* • Campsite by river • Fly fishing • Hiking trails • Wolves howling • Spotted grizzly bear	• History Teacher • Woodworking • Shop outside with two long tables in center of room. • On the outer edges of walls, there were lower cabinets. • Above the cabinets was a pegboard with tools. Tools are labeled in their spots. • Power tools were kept in lower cabinets.

Discussion with Group or Partner About the Process or Exercise:

1. Were you able to hold your power for the full reading? Did you drop into the psychic? What can you do to help yourself for the next reading?
2. Was it easy or difficult for you to decide which pieces of evidence would be a good choice to dig a little deeper into? Did the recipient nudge you?

3. Were you able to unfold more information from one piece of evidence?
4. How is the blending or moving into the evidence going? Are you able to get at least three more bits to add to the original evidence?
5. What areas will you work on and improve for future readings?
6. What questions do you have for your spirit team?

Journal Reflection:

- Reflect on how you feel about your reading today. Write your thoughts down.
- Share any emotions or struggles that may have come up.
- What were your strengths? Where did you have challenges?
- What was your gold nugget, the best bit of the reading?
- Close your eyes, take a few deep breaths, and ask your soul what wisdom it wants to leave with you today. Wait for it to come. Start writing.

I have no special talent. I am only passionately curious.

—Albert Einstein

Chapter 8

"The Wow Factor"

My goal is to bring The Wow Factor into my readings. For me, Wow! evidence is when the recipient or the audience gasps—or when someone starts to cry. That's when you know you have touched the soul of your recipient. Striving to become a medium who brings through a lot of Wow evidence is not about ego or finding fame—it's about the healing that happens between two worlds as you touch a soul. If you're working with an audience, even when only a few participants receive a message, Wow evidence can touch the souls of all who attend.

How to Obtain "The Wow Factor"

To help us reach The Wow Factor in our mediumship, I believe there are three key shifts we can make. The first is to "delve deeper into the evidence." Be passionately curious. Dig a little deeper to find the gold nuggets of the communicator's life. Once you've mastered delving deeper, you can move into the next shift: Allowing the communicator's life to unfold through the art of storytelling. The last shift is touching the souls of those listening to the reading.

Delve Deeper

I always thought my goal as a medium was to give as much evidence as possible, both to support the progression of the communicator's soul after its life on Earth, and to show the sitter that I really did have their loved one with me. It was as if I was racing against the clock—"How many pieces of evidence can I get?" On a good day, I could get thirty or more pieces of evidence in a platform demonstration. Oh, after those contacts, I would ruffle up my feathers, throw my chest out, and walk back to my seat proudly. I thought I was doing wonderful work with all that evidence. Little did I know at the time; less evidence equals more evidence. It's far more effective to take a few key pieces of evidence, then delve a little deeper. Are there any hidden pieces to bring forward? Remember, the life of any seventy-five-year-old has a wealth of hidden stories— just imagine all their life events! Let's not be complacent, giving just personality traits, their manner of passing, bringing forward only a few details from the last few years of their life, or giving random pieces of evidence that don't connect to form a cohesive story. Plumb the depths ... dive down to find the buried tales ... probe the story of your communicator's life ... discover The Wow Factor.

I like using the analogy of an iceberg to show what we often do as mediums. At water level, we see only a tiny portion of an iceberg. To get the full effect of the size and beauty of an iceberg, we have to plunge down into the ocean. Mediumship is the same. We often stay above water, touching only the surface of the evidence. To find the best parts of the evidence, we need to dive in and uncover the beauty of the story begging to be told. Think of "surface evidence" as a treasure chest delivered from the spirit world. Unfasten the latch. Open the chest. Dig deep inside. What jewels can you discover?

I often have readings with mediums and my father frequently comes through. Each time, the medium will bring through evidence similar to evidence other mediums have brought in. Let's look at a few graphics with typical evidence I have received from various mediums in regard to my dad in the spirit world and then look at the evidence that is hidden beneath the surface.

In this graphic, you can see the iceberg, its tip, and the enormous size of the submerged part. Think of the tip of the iceberg as representing the bits of information readily known to most people in our inner and outer circle of friends and family. As noted above, I call this "surface evidence"—but some people might call it "vague evidence."

This tip-of-the-iceberg type of evidence works well in a one-to-one reading—but it could get you into trouble in an audience setting if this is all you give. Why? In a demonstration, many people will understand most surface evidence, so you can't just "throw it out" to the audience at large, you have to take it directly to a recipient. As noted earlier, if you throw it out, many people will raise their hands, wanting to make the evidence fit their contact or loved one.

Also, notice how tip-of-the-iceberg evidence is random. There is nothing cohesive there, nothing thematic that forms a story about the communicator—the evidence is just there, like tiny pieces of ice floating in the middle of a vast ocean. This is what I used to do and thought I was doing really well. I should say "Really well, for a beginner." This is what we all do when we first start out. We're like little gulls floating above the ocean looking for a place to land. But the day comes when you flap your wings a little harder because a big iceberg just floated into view.

Staying with my dad's evidence, the next step is to look at all the pieces of evidence and decide: "Which pieces are key? Which ones can I delve into? Which ones will help me form a story?" In the graphic below, notice that there are stars next to four pieces of evidence about my dad. If I were the medium in that reading, I would want to know more about these four pieces.

Let's take a look at the next graphic to see what it might look like to delve deeper into each of these pieces of evidence.

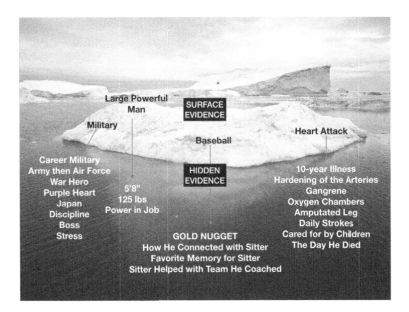

Notice how the evidence becomes more personal. Now we are getting into the true essence of my dad. Looking at his military career, we see that this man accomplished great things. The evidence shows that he held a position of power—and when that sense of power comes through to mediums, they often interpret it as referring to his physical stature. In fact, my father was a small man—with a formidable energy that resonated through him because of the job he did. The job stress led to his long, ten-year illness and its related ups and downs. There are so many story directions one could go with the story of Dad's illness. But it all comes down to this: My father's powerful persona dwindled; he declined over time until he had to be hand-fed and helped with every aspect of his life. There were a lot of hardships during that time, but you know, hidden among them are some very funny stories too—and when you as the medium "delve deep," those stories will come to the fore.

The evidence also shows that Dad's heart attack was merely a symptom of a complicated illness. He suffered from this illness for ten years, it was a huge part of his life. It changed his whole persona—and through the resulting physical limitations, he lost his power.

You may wonder, "How do these four pieces of evidence connect to form a cohesive story?" Let's take a look at the next graphic.

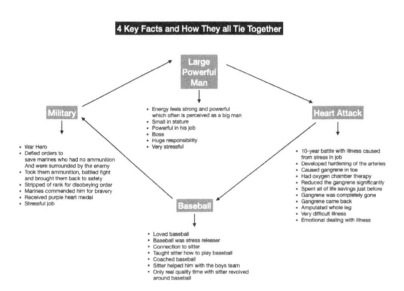

It doesn't matter which piece of evidence you start with; each will lead to the next. If I were the medium, the most logical place to begin would be either with the military aspect or with Dad's heart attack.

Let's imagine that our medium chooses to start with the military facet of Dad's life and, delving deep, then chooses to work with one particular piece of evidence: the war hero. The military connection leads some mediums to interpret my father as a "large, powerful man." But again, that sense comes from all the responsibility on his shoulders and the authority of the role he held in his job. This evidence shows Dad's depth of character. At one stage in Dad's story, he had known that the enemy was drawing close to the Marines' position. Despite orders not to go, he snuck out in the middle of the night to take them ammunition. Shortly after he arrived at their camp, there was a battle. All the Marines and my father survived because they had what they needed to fight the enemy. His moral compass would not allow him to leave the Marines to die; to him, it wasn't right. He risked his life to bring them back to safety. This is a great example of why we should delve into the evidence given to find the hidden story. Imagine how I would feel to hear a medium share this courageous fact about Dad!

You can also see in the evidence that baseball was a special memory for the sitter: *me*. Of course, as a medium, this is where you'd want to go ... because this will tug at the sitter's heart strings.

Baseball was the one thing my father loved. He was a busy man—being called away at all times of the night, working crazy hours—it was hard to find time to be with him. Baseball created that time. When Dad was the coach of my brother's team, I travelled with him often, and he would designate me "the helper." I was in charge of managing the score book and making sure the boys on the team knew the batting order. Those times were special. Want to make me cry in a reading? Bring up baseball with my dad.

Here's the thing: For the titles Military, Larger Powerful Man, Baseball, and Heart Attack listed in the image titled "4 Key Facts and How They All Tie Together" above, you could easily break away, delving deep into each of those topics to bring forward even more detailed evidence.

For example, there's a scary story that goes with Dad's amputation. Once, he needed to go to Dallas to have a fitting for his prosthetic leg. I was scheduled to pick him up around 8:30 in the morning to drive him to Dallas. I dropped my kids off at school and headed to his house. When I arrived, he was gone, and so was his old, beat up pickup truck. Panic set in. Dad was not mentally or physically able to drive. To make matters worse, the truck had faulty steering and was hard to keep on the road.

I phoned Mom at work. "Get on the highway," she said. "He probably set off to Dallas on his own. See if you can catch up to him."

Dallas was two hours away. I stopped and picked a friend up just in case I did find him and needed someone to drive my car back. I was terrified I would find Dad in a ditch—or worse, in a wreck on the highway.

Once we got to Dallas, I saw Dad driving on an eight-lane freeway—travelling in the opposite direction from me! Cars were swerving to miss him. My heart sank. Terrified, I veered into the far right-hand lane to exit. It took a few minutes to get turned around and headed in the same direction as Dad but finally I caught up to him. I pulled up beside him, honking the horn to get his attention. After what seemed like eternity, he recognized me. He was happy to see me, his eyes lit up, and a big smile crossed his face. He pulled over. I jumped out of my car and ran to his. Opening the driver side door, I motioned for him to scoot over. To my surprise, he did.

Dad had no idea what he had done. He was confused. I broke down in tears. I was so relieved he was alive, grateful he had not been in a wreck, and grateful I had spotted him on the other side of the road in heavy morning traffic.

At that moment, our roles changed. I was no longer the daughter. I was the parent. Dad was no longer the parent, he was the child. I scolded him for taking off without me. Yes, I did. He needed to know the importance of waiting the next time. It was the look on his face, though—that look a child gives you when they know they have been saved. That look they give you when they are scared to death and mom or dad comes to the rescue. Only in this case, it was the parent giving the child that look. It broke my heart yet at the same time, melted it.

We laugh at this story—it was so like Dad to pull a stunt like this—and bless his heart, cognitively, he had no idea what a panic he'd caused.

Each piece of evidence listed above is my dad's story, beginning with him as a young man in war and spanning the arc of his life to include his last ten years. There's practical evidence, we feel his essence and his character, and The Wow Factor is there too. If a medium were to give me a reading, touching on some of what is shown, as the sitter I would walk away sobbing, overjoyed.

I know this is a lot of specific evidence. *Don't panic.* You're not expected to give detailed readings every time—but this shows you that you could choose one of the four pieces of evidence, dive into it, and give an entire reading on just that one piece. The possibilities are endless—and so is your potential as a medium!

I believe that the deeper you go into a communicator's story, the more you touch those involved, and the more you create change or healing. So, why not strive to go as deep as you can? The worst thing that could happen is that you might focus on only a few pieces of evidence. But even a few is better than settling for surface evidence. Take the dive!

Go for the Gold

I was in London participating in an all-day workshop and was asked to make a contact in front of the group. A woman came forward from the spirit world. She was a stern, serious woman with a great deal of power. The more I worked with her, the more I became aware of her being from another country. She felt Chinese. I also became aware of her being a part of the government and that she was often in the presence of foreign dignitaries. Her work involved making serious decisions that could be life-altering for many people. She was no ordinary woman and her story was incredible—I just had to go with it and let it unfold.

But that's the thing—surrender to the spirit world and they will bring you amazing evidence, evidence that is so "out there," it's hard to believe. Implausible or unusual evidence is *great* evidence—especially when you are working with an audience and you need to find your recipient quickly.

"But," you might ask, "Can we make amazing evidence happen?" Of course, we can't make those in the spirit world do anything they don't want to do, but we can develop ourselves so the spirit world can bring us this type of evidence easily. If you offer the spirit world a treasure trove of ways to work with you, that precious, sparkling evidence will begin to drop in when you least expect it. So, surrender to your communicator and spread those wonderful gems from the spirit world around!

The Perfect Combination

I recently gave a reading from a father to his daughter. The father had not been in the spirit world long and was excited to speak with his daughter again. The first piece of evidence he shared was of his dog. The daughter smiled and nodded. I could have left that piece of evidence just as it appeared: *a dog*. I had my "Yes" from the daughter—but something inside me said "Delve deeper."

I moved my energy into the image of the dog and the story began to unfold. I could see a dog of medium build, he felt like a hunting dog. When I said "hunting dog," more images flooded into my mind—they were moving so fast, it was all I could do to stay ahead of the evidence.

Before I knew it, I was on a mind journey with this father and his beloved dog. I felt the tall grasses in the fields reaching as high as the knee. The air was crisp, the wind was blowing gently, I could hear birds flying overhead. I became aware of the father searching the sky for a particular bird. He wasn't interested in the large white birds off in the distance. He wanted the ducks: mallards.

A shot rang through the air, a bird fell to the ground. The father motioned for his dog to retrieve the bird. The dog stood at attention. The father yelled, "Go on, go get the bird." The dog looked back at his owner and sat down. What transpired next was funny. This poor father and his beloved hunting dog were replaying a scene that happened time and again. The dog would never retrieve the birds. He was trained to do it, but he wouldn't leave the father's side. The father took the leash and walked the dog to the downed bird. The dog picked the bird up and pranced proudly back to the car.

The father loved his dog and took him hunting often. It was the family joke: That dog wouldn't do what he was trained to do. The father didn't care. All that mattered to him was the time he spent with his dog.

I love this story. Everything came together just as it was meant to. I was given the image of the dog, I blended into the image, and a beautiful story of a father and his beloved hunting dog unfolded. After many years of separation, this father was now reunited with his dog. This is what delving deeper looks like. This whole story began with *one image*. The recipient did not expect to hear this story—it brought her joy and touched her soul as she went down memory lane with her father.

From Russia with Love

In the first circle I sat in, a fellow medium brought through a spirit family for a man in our circle; they wanted to share important information with him. The man was in the middle of uncovering his family history and was running into a few snags. He was part of an important Russian family; his grandparents and great grandparents had escaped their country. Their lives had been in danger, they'd lived many months on the run, hiding on the land and in abandoned buildings.

They hid family jewels and heirlooms along the way. They came to give the recipient information about towns the family had hidden in while on the run. They gave him valuable information regarding family documents. We were all engrossed in the story as it unfolded, and so was the recipient! He had new information to help him on his quest. This could easily have been an ordinary reading. But the medium who gave the reading decided to "delve a little deeper" and allow the story to unfold, bringing through some incredible evidence.

For me the perfect combination is when the essence of the communicator shines through. As the evidence unfolds the story, the spirit world are happy with the reading and the recipient has been uplifted in some way.

Pulling it All Together

What are the biggest issues for me in delving deep to receive The Wow Factor evidence in my readings? Firstly: *Trust.* It's so easy to say the word, yet it's challenging to really trust yourself. Secondly, I found that using my strongest clairs—clairvoyance and clairsentience—in every reading got in my way. I became so comfortable using them, I often ignored evidence coming to me in a different way. I had to become mindful of all of my clairs, bringing together clairaudience, claircognizance, clairgustance, and clairalience; unfolding elements of storytelling and mind journeys; and delving deeper. My readings started to take off. Everything began to click and roll along smoothly. I worked relentlessly on all of these aspects until finally it all came together.

Hard work pays off, that's for sure. I didn't just watch the tip of the iceberg float by ... I dove in and experienced the ninety-five percent beneath the surface. In the process, I brought forward exciting, inspiring, and heart-warming evidence from the spirit world and made a difference in my sitter's life. That's *The Wow Factor.*

Exercise 1

The Wow Factor

Objective:

The aim of this exercise is to move toward The Wow Factor evidence your recipient would recognize.

Type of Reading:

To get a good grasp on how to bring it all together, I recommend doing all these readings as one- to-one sittings. If you can bring a group of people together or you are working in a circle, you may practice them in group or gallery settings. For the purpose of this exercise, one-to-one settings are fifteen to thirty minutes long; gallery-style readings are seven to ten minutes long.

Materials Needed:

- Device to record your reading.
- Journal.
- Handout – The Wow Factor.
- Video – The Wow Factor (Optional).

Number of Participants:

- Two or more.

Table #16: Expectations: The Wow Factor

Expectations	
Medium's Role	**Recipient's Role**
• Connect with the spirit world. • Hold your power for the length of the reading. • Intent is to bring through evidence that will leave the spirit world and recipient satisfied. Touching the soul of the sitter is a bonus. • Bring The Wow Factor in by allowing the spirit communicator to tell the story. • Get five key pieces of evidence from the spirit communicator before starting your reading. Aim to get a piece of evidence using each clair: see, hear, feel, know, smell, and taste. • Delve deep on key pieces of evidence to weave a story.	• The sitter is the time-keeper. Please let the medium know when they've exceeded their time. • Feedback should consist of "Yes," "No," "I don't know," or "I'm not sure." • No additional feedback is necessary. • If the medium touches on a key piece of evidence, you may stop them and say, "Go deeper on the evidence you just gave."

Procedures:

1. Set your intent.
2. Hit "Record" on your phone or recorder.
3. Do the reading.
4. Stop recording.

Handout:

Table #17: The Wow Factor – Exercise

Wow Factor Exercise				
Before you begin your reading, set your intent to receive one piece of evidence from each of the clairs. Then connect with your spirit communicator and as the evidence comes, write it down under the correct column. If you receive more than one piece of evidence for a category or no evidence for a category, it's okay. Record what you get.				
List Images	List What You Hear	List What You Feel	List What You Know	List What You Smell or Taste

Example of what this exercise might look like.

Table #18: The Wow Factor – Exercise – Example #1

Wow Factor Exercise Example				
Before you begin your reading, set your intent to receive one piece of evidence from each of the clairs. Then connect with your spirit communicator and as the evidence comes, write it down under the correct column. If you receive more than one piece of evidence for a category or no evidence for a category, it's okay. Record what you get.				
List Images	List What You Hear	List What You Feel	List What You Know	List What You Smell or Taste
Front Porch Clock	Laughter	Love	Apple of his eye	Smell oranges

From this handout, the following story could emerge from the evidence.

Table #19: The Wow Factor – Exercise – Example #2

Wow Factor Exercise Example				
List Images	List Images	List What You Feel	List What You Know	List What You Smell or Taste
Above the heater, sitting on a shelf, was an antique clock made of wood.

The clock had been broken for years.

No one could fix it, though many had tried.

Sitter now has the clock.

It chimes randomly now but the hands on the clock don't move. | There were two porches in the communicator's house.

Front porch and back porch.

People were always stopping by to sit and chat on either porch.

The back porch had an old rocking chair.

The spirit communicator would often rock the sitter while in the rocking chair.

The sitter now owns the rocking chair. | The love of this man for his family is strong.

There was always plenty of hugs, laughs, and love to go around.

He would help anyone in need.

He showed his love for others by helping.

There was a lot of love shared sitting on the porches.

Sitter was the apple of this man's eye. | Sitter was the apple of this man's eye. | Spirit communicator's favorite candy was orange slices.

He always had a fresh supply in a crystal bowl next to his chair.

Sitter has memory of sitting on spirit communicator's lap eating the orange candies with him. |

Discussion with Group or Partner About the Process or Exercise:

Take a look at the handout together.

1. Were you able to bring evidence forward that the sitter wanted?
2. If yes, were you able to go deep within the evidence?
3. Were there any pieces of evidence in which the sitter was able to coach you to go deeper?
4. If yes, were you able to go deeper?
5. Did a story begin to form from your evidence? If yes, which parts were key? If no, what could you have done differently?

Journal:

- How are you feeling about today's exercise?
- Did any emotions or struggles come up in the exercise?
- What were your strengths? Where did you have challenges? Write these down.
- What was your "gold nugget" ... the best bit of the reading?
- Close your eyes, take a few deep breaths, and ask your soul what wisdom it wants to leave with you today. Wait for it to come. Have fun and start writing!

The more willing you are to surrender to the energy within you, the more power can flow through you.

—Shakti Gawain

CHAPTER 9

"MULTIPLE COMMUNICATORS"

I remember the first time I saw a tutor at the College bring through multiple communicators for multiple recipients scattered throughout the audience. I sat there, mouth wide open in disbelief. It was amazing. "Will I ever get to that stage?" I thought. "Will I eventually learn to do that?" I couldn't wait! But first I needed to learn to work with multiple communicators and just one recipient. So, I put that thought out to my spirit team and waited for the opportunity to arrive.

Not long after that I was on a course with the same tutor. I was with a small group of students in the back of the sanctuary. It was my turn to give a reading, I was nervous, but I stood and began the reading. I had a woman in spirit, she was joined quickly by another woman, her sister. I had a moment of panic—I had two communicators—but at the same time it was exhilarating! I didn't know what to do. I wasn't about to ask the tutor for help, I was too shy, too unsure of myself. (I know ... not wanting help when I needed it the most!) So, I said to myself, "Okay this is what you've been given. Now make it work."

I ended up having the mother on my left and the aunt on my right. How this happened I don't know. Perhaps my friends in high places helped me out a bit. All I know is it worked—but it was not pretty. I knew who was speaking to me by how the direction of the energy felt. If it came from my left, it was the mother. If it came from my right, it was the aunt. It was so exciting ... I found myself hopping from my left foot to my right, moving my body to match the energy moving to and fro. Looking back, it must have been quite comical. Picture an uncoordinated person wearing clown shoes learning new dance steps, enjoying every minute of the dance but looking ridiculous. That was me. Awkward but overly excited, not really caring what I looked like—because I had two communicators at the same time!

So, I carried on a conversation with both communicators simultaneously. Their personalities shone through; their fun bickering back and forth was how they were in life. The recipient laughed and laughed to see her mom and aunt carrying on as if they were still alive.

Oh my, guys, I was on fire. I couldn't wait to do it again. Later, I continued to bring multiple communicators through. It was exciting then and it still is today. I am more graceful now, though—I've ditched the clown shoes.

Moving on Up

One mentorship weekend, the tutor asked, "Would anyone like to bring through multiple communicators with multiple recipients?" Totally out of character, I raised my hand—and shocked myself. I loved the feeling of working with multiple communicators so much, I couldn't wait to try bringing in two communicators for two different recipients.

I walked to the front, stepped into my power. I could feel two communicators right away. One communicator stepped forward and I began. I established who the recipient was (on the right side of the room) and then felt the second communicator step forward as the first stepped back. I gave a few pieces of evidence and found my recipient (on the left side of the room). I moved between the two communicators in the same way I had done on that day in the back of the sanctuary—well, sort of. I wasn't clunking around as much. It was more like moving slowly from one side of the room to the other as I worked with one communicator and recipient, switching when the time was right. To say that I was beyond excited wouldn't come close to how I truly felt after that contact. According to my mentor, however, I was not quite up to par. I listened to her every word. I walked away knowing my delivery was a bit awkward, maybe even a bit controlling, and I definitely needed to surrender more and blend more deeply. Back in my seat, I processed it all, allowing her critique to permeate my being. I had a lot of work to do to get where I wanted but I couldn't have been more proud of what I had just done.

Separating Communicators

Before I began training with my mentor or going to the College, I would sit in my living room and create exercises in my mind for me to do with my guides. My guides were my teachers. I didn't really have anyone to practice with back then; it was just me and them. I would ask my guide to stand near me and would decide where he was standing. Was he behind me, to the left, to the right, or in front of me? Once I was good at detecting where he was, I'd asked him to move farther from me and then I'd do the same thing. The next goal was for two or more spirits to come into the room, and to determine where they were standing—sometimes they were close to me, sometimes farther away.

This became my morning routine—sometimes before my feet touched the floor. Upon waking, I would become aware of someone in the corner of my room. I would decide who they were, then make my way downstairs. I was always greeted by family and friends in the spirit world. As I walked in I would greet each of them and point out where they were around the room. I'd feel a subtle shift of energy when someone moved to a new place. I can't tell you for sure that this worked but I can say that I've never had trouble distinguishing where spirit communicators around me are or knowing which direction a communication is coming from. I feel the energy. In the beginning, it was doing this exercise that helped me find a way to engage in a dialogue with multiple communicators. Perhaps this is why on that first day in the back of the sanctuary, the spirit communicators separated on their own. Maybe my spirit team and I had practiced so many times that the process shifted into the real deal without a hitch. So, I recommend that you do these exercises too, on your own or with a partner. It doesn't matter who comes in from the spirit world, I always left it up to my guide to decide.

Timing

Working in this way is about timing and where you are in your development. Mediumship development is not a sprint, it's a marathon. It's important to allow your development to unfold naturally. Let's not be in a hurry. Learn how to work with one communicator at a time and do it well before attempting multiples. Chat with your spirit team to see how they feel. Trust that they know exactly the right time to bring in multiple communicators, and when to work with multiple communicators and multiple recipients simultaneously.

Energy

I'm always asked, "How do you know when you have more than one communicator?" For me it's feeling the subtle differences, the shift of energy. The exercise I mentioned earlier taught me a lot about subtle shifts of energy, I could feel spirit moving in and out of my space when I began working with multiple communicators. I could feel which direction the evidence was coming from, which told me who was speaking. We as mediums must pay attention to everything happening around us while we work. It's not just about gathering evidence from the spirit world. We need to understand *how* the spirit world is working with us so we can feel them moving in and out during a reading. Understanding energy, how it works, and how it feels is the path to building a solid foundation as you journey toward working with multiple communicators.

Three Husbands, Three Wives

I was working in a church in New Market, United Kingdom one day and I had three husbands show up all at once. In the past, I had brought through two communicators for two recipients at the same time but never three at the same time. The three wives were all sitting across the back rows on either side of the room. I began the reading with one woman by establishing her husband, moved to the second and established her husband, and then did the same for the third wife.

All three husbands began with a single rose. This was the common thread that brought the three husbands together. The color of each rose and the story behind it was different for each wife, that's how I was able to separate the three. I continued working, bringing through some lovely evidence (and some healing too, as one had only just lost her husband). It was my last reading so I thanked the women and sat down. As soon as I sat down, I heard subjectively, loud and clear, "You forgot one." I closed my eyes and sighed. Oh my, I did forget. I never went back to the third husband after establishing his identity. The rest of the reading had been for the other two women. I felt awful.

I spoke to the three women afterward and apologized to one wife for leaving her husband standing in the distance waiting for his turn to speak again. She thought it was funny and said it didn't matter because some of what I had said to the other two women resonated with her and her husband. I still felt bad. I learned that through their grief, these three women had become friends. They'd meet once a week for coffee to support one another.

I wanted to tell you this story so I could share what the service chairperson told me after the service. She was a medium, knew a lot about energy, and had watched my energy as I worked with these three husbands. I had one husband on each side of me, one in the back, and I could feel them as I was working. She saw my energy moving and changing with each communicator. She said that as one stepped forward, my energy changed colors on my right side. When that communicator stepped back, the colors changed, and when the one on the left stepped forward, the colors changed again. She said it was like watching a beautiful, orchestrated dance of colors. She could see me leaning into their energy as they moved in and shifting my energy to the other side when they moved out.

This is what happens when you work with multiples. You dance between communicators and recipients, weaving a story for each. My experience has been that multiple-link communicators usually have a thread of similarity that links them together. That similarity gets me started. In this case, it was the rose—but it could be anything. I enjoy pointing out how my communicators are similar and then bringing in their differences. For example, both of two communicators might love riding bikes but one rides bikes on paved roads for long distance trips and the other prefers rugged cross-country bike adventures.

I wish I could give you a magic formula to make this all work for you, but if there is a formula, I am unaware of it. I can share my experiences so you have an idea ... the rest is up to you and your spiritual team. When the time is right, explore with your team and try different methods until you find one that is right for you.

I don't know if all mediums are able to work in this way, and this method is definitely for the advanced medium. If you can bounce between multiple communicators for one recipient easily, then perhaps this is something your team will want to try with you. Don't force it, though. It will come when you are ready.

Tips for Working with Multiple Communicators

Working with multiple communicators is tricky. We all seem to want to get there far sooner than we are spiritually developed for—or ready for. Trusting our spirit team to bring more than one loved one through at the right time is important. We can ask for it to happen in our practice sessions but when we are working with a client, we have to let it happen naturally. There are a few things you can do to make the process a little easier:

- Wait for it to happen as a natural progression in your development.
- Separate each communicator so you know their placement. You can have one communicator step forward at a time, or you can have one on each side of you. Work with your spirit team to see what works best for you.

- Begin with one communicator at a time. For example, have Dad come in first and work with him. Then, have him step back and have Mom come through.
- Establish the identity of each communicator as they enter the conversation, by sharing evidence that reveals their identity.
- Balance the essence of each communicator (such as personality) with the practical evidence (such as shared memories).
- Surrender: It's a must with multiple communicators.
- Work toward weaving a story. This is easier said than done with multiples. Give it time.
- Give a message at the end of the reading if you feel drawn to do so. Messages are often woven into the evidence.

"Meeting the Needs"

Many of my tutors at the Arthur Findlay College talked about "Meeting the needs of the recipient and the spirit communicator." But what does that mean? To be honest, for a long time in my early years, the only needs I thought about were mine: Connect with the spirit world and bring evidence through. In the beginning of our development, that's normal.

As I began to understand the spirit world and my role as the medium, the meaning of the phrase "meeting the needs" started to click with me. In my training with one tutor, I learned to do a quick scan of the sitter in a one-to-one reading: What did their soul need? Was their soul crying out for direction in their life? Was it yearning to hear from a departed loved one? Based on what their soul revealed, I'd proceed with the reading.

Working on a soul-to-soul level and meeting the needs of the soul is what we do. But we have to be mindful of balancing the needs of those in the physical world and those in the spirit world. For example, in a one-to-one reading once, as I scanned my sitter, I saw that this woman's soul was crying out for direction. But she insisted I make a contact with the spirit world. I posed a few questions to make sure I understood what she wanted and obliged. A gentleman from the spirit world joined us; I could feel him standing behind me. Once I established who he was, he went into a message about her current life. Once he had opened the door to her life, I dipped into the psychic and worked with her. In the end, the reading helped her and she was satisfied—she'd heard from the gentleman she'd hoped to hear from. But we met her soul's needs too. She'd needed to hear the things I would have told her (had I worked only on a psychic level) directly from this gentleman.

The Spirit World's Needs

Linking into the sitter to decide the needs of the soul is simple. But how do we go about meeting the needs of the spirit world? As noted earlier, I believe we meet the needs of the spirit world or our communicator by surrendering to the spirit world, blending with the communicator, delving into the evidence, and allowing the spirit communicator to take the lead.

Imagine yourself in the spirit world. You have one chance to communicate with your loved ones through a medium: *one chance*. You have to get it right. You have to say what you need to say ... whether it is to heal or to uplift or simply to reassure your loved one that you are okay.

You begin working with a medium but the medium has a list of items to go through first. The medium makes you jump through hoops, answering the questions on their List. By the time you've answered all their questions, that special moment has been lost. You may never get another chance. Your spirit communicator knows far more about the sitter than you the medium know; they have memories with the sitter. You don't. They know what story needs telling and what words need to be spoken to meet the needs of their loved one and themselves. So, it makes sense to allow them to take the lead, to tell their story. This is their moment, not yours. Your role is to serve spirit. You do that by allowing your communicator to weave their story, bringing encouragement, empowerment, or healing to the recipient.

Adding Depth

Spirit never comes alone. Working with multiple communicators adds depth to your readings, and there are always others hoping to come through from the spirit world too. Once you are strong at working with one communicator, I recommend working with multiples for one recipient ... work with your first communicator, then bring in the second and third. Once you can do this well, experiment with working with two communicators simultaneously, going back and forth between the two. It's just like being in a conversation. From there, work your way toward carrying on conversations with multiple communicators at the same time. This is a great way to bring the true essence of your communicators through.

Recently, I brought through a family who was playing dominos in the spirit world. As I worked with them, they were all speaking to me and as they played their game, I brought through their conversation. It was great confirmation for the recipients to hear their family members carrying on just as they had here on earth, drinking their favorite beverages, and gossiping about all the happenings in the family.

When you are working with an audience, bringing through multiple communicators with multiple recipients adds excitement to the demonstration. It keeps the audience on their toes as they keep up with multiple stories unfolding. As a medium, this is my favorite thing to do when working with an audience, but I can't force it to happen. In fact, I never know if it will. I allow spirit to decide.

Have patience, it will all come together at the right time. Remember to pay attention to the subtle shifts in energy around you while working.

Exercise 1

Multiple Communicators

Objective:

The objective of this exercise is to practice working with more than one communicator so you can learn to feel the subtle shifts as they move in and out of your auric field.

Type of Reading:

I recommend doing all these readings as one-to-one sittings both psychically and mediumistically, to get a good grasp on how to bring it all together. You may practice them in group or gallery settings using mediumistic faculties if you can get extra people or are working in a circle. One-to-one sittings are fifteen to thirty minutes long for the purpose of a practice exercise. Gallery style readings are seven to ten minutes long.

Materials Needed:

- Device to record your reading.
- Journal.
- Handout – Multiple Communicators.
- Video – Multiple Communicators (Optional).

Number of Participants:

- Two or more.

Table #20: Expectations: Multiple Communicators

Expectations: Multiple Communicators	
Medium's Role	**Recipient's Role**
• Set your intention to work with more than one communicator. • Connect with the spirit world. • Begin your reading. • If you feel more than one spirit communicator, ask one to step back. Let them know you'll work with them next. • Pay attention to the subtle shifts in energy as one steps forward and one steps back. • Establish who each communicator is, giving evidence to support your claim as they move in to work with you. • Once you have established who the communicator is and given a few practical pieces of evidence, you can ask them to step back and have a new communicator step forward.	• The sitter is the time keeper. Please let the medium know when they've exceeded their time. • Feedback should consist of "Yes," "No," "I don't know," or "I'm not sure." • No additional feedback is necessary.

Procedures:

1. Set your intent to work with multiple communicators.
2. Hit "Record" on your phone or recorder.
3. Do the reading.
4. Stop recording.

Discussion with Group or Partner About the Process or Exercise:

1. Were you able to feel the subtle shifts in energy?
2. Did you know a new communicator had stepped forward in a different way?
3. How did it go moving between two communicators? Was it difficult? Was it a smooth transition?
4. What goal do you have for moving forward with this task? Should you keep practicing or should you wait until you're more solid with blending and surrendering?
5. What were you most proud of during the reading?

Journal:

*   Reflect on how you feel about your reading today. Write down your thoughts.
*   Share any emotions or struggles that may have come up.
*   What were your strengths? Where did you have challenges? Write these down.
*   What was your gold nugget, the best bit of the reading?
*   Close your eyes, take a few deep breaths and ask your soul what wisdom it wants to leave with you today. Wait for it to come and start writing.

In our struggle for freedom,
truth is the only weapon we possess.

—The Dalai Lama

Chapter 10

"Assessments"

In mediumship training, assessments help you see the progress you are making over a period of time and help you discover your strengths and weaknesses. But most of us (if we are honest) don't like assessments or being subjected to any type of test. I'm no different—I hated tests in school, I never did well with them.

In my mediumship development, I did my fair share of assessing my progress. At first, it was hard to listen to myself, and in the earliest recordings, I cringed at what I heard. But then I'd listen to my latest recording and was amazed at how much my mediumship had transformed. I could see easily where my biggest growth areas were and where I needed to keep working.

Let's Get Serious

Let's get serious for a moment. If you are a true medium, mediumship is a calling. No matter how much you try to ignore it or run from it, it will always come back around, you'll feel that pull to learn more. If this sounds like you, you're likely taking every course, reading every book, and you can't get enough. Am I right? That's how it was for me. Once I made up my mind to study mediumship and stop ignoring that calling, I had tunnel vision. All I could see in front of me was mediumship. I was on a mission, I wanted to turn it upside down, sideways, inside out, and shake it. What else was there for me to learn? It was important for me to understand why this was happening, how it was happening, and how could I use it to help others.

Find a Tutor Who Speaks to Your Soul

I searched for the perfect tutor. I wanted a tutor who touched my soul and I found that special touch with Mavis Pittilla. My soul overflows when I am in her presence. Her wisdom speaks to me in ways no other tutor's words have done. I urge you to find a mentor who touches your soul in the same way. It is important.

I was fortunate to live in England where many highly-trained mediums live. As I look back at how it all unfolded, I see that it all fell into my lap in the most unexpected ways: One amazing tutor led me to my mentor and my mentor led me to other amazing tutors. I would pinch myself sometimes and ask, "Am I living in a dream?" How lucky I was to end up in England surrounded by such knowledgeable mediums!

As I mentioned earlier, I took three fifteen-month mentorship programs with Mavis, and I wanted to continue to learn with others between our scheduled mentorships. I wanted my tutors to have trained with Gordon Higginson or with another of Gordon's students. I knew that if I did this, their philosophy would be like Mavis'. Of course, their teaching styles varied; each tutor put their own spin on each topic. As an educator, I found immense value in observing how each teacher's instruction style and philosophical views lined up or differed. I knew that being mindful of the diversity of approaches would both help me as a medium and—if I ever had the inclination to do so—as teacher of mediumship.

As you choose mentors or teachers for your own development, I caution you about studying with multiple teachers whose philosophy is not compatible. Why? Because conflicting viewpoints can be confusing. Who is right? I was careful to choose tutors whose philosophy on mediumship was almost the same, so the slight differences didn't create any huge issues. Please keep this in mind.

My Training

My training was fast, furious, and hard. I studied with Mavis and with a few other tutors at the College, and I took a monthly class in London with another tutor from the College. I didn't have a moment to breathe. I put my life on hold to learn mediumship. I don't expect you or anyone else to do what I did … and I wouldn't recommend it … I was a bit crazy for five years. I had no other responsibilities other than work so I threw myself into my studies.

When I was a kid, my momma would always ask me, "Are you okay with being average or do you want to rise to the top?" I wanted to rise to the top. It was non-negotiable. I chose tutors who took mediumship training seriously. They pushed me, stretched me, and flipped me upside down. Some days my head would spin as I tried to take it all in and make sense of what I was learning. If I was going to be a medium, I had to be the best I could be. I'm not there yet. I'm a student for life—there's always something more you can learn or do to improve.

Recordings

When I worked as a reading specialist in the education system, I often recorded my young students reading so they could hear how they sounded. For most children, it was the only way for them to grasp the concept of reading fluently. In their minds, they were already reading fluently—but in reality, they sounded like robots. Listening to themselves reading helped them in many ways, and once a month, we would do a recording to see if we could hear growth. Their little faces would light up when they heard their reading styles changing from robotic to dynamic.

Just as I did with my students, Mavis would have us record our readings, we'd listen to them, and we'd analyze our strengths and weaknesses. I dreaded that process. It was hard watching myself on video giving a reading or demonstrating and in the beginning, I struggled to find any strengths. I noticed every single mistake I made and saw only failure. I'd have a good cry over a glass of wine or two and then remember what it was like for my little students to hear their reading improving. I would say to myself, "Girl, you are no different. One day, you too will see improvement. One day, you too will smile when you watch your videos." Then I'd hear my momma's words in my head saying, "Are you okay with being mediocre? Or are you someone who rises to the top?" So, I'd put my big girl pants on, pick myself up, and carry on.

Self-Analysis

One of the tasks required in my mentorships with Mavis was to record our readings and do a self-analysis using special forms. We would turn the forms in as homework assignments and the tutor would have a look. Sometimes we had to turn in the videos as well. Three readings with three recordings and an analysis of each was a typical assignment between class meetings. We did so many recordings, it became second nature and at some point, I must have moved beyond seeing only what I did wrong because when I listened back, I marked myself as having done well. Actually, I marked myself as having done really well. I would turn my self-assessments in proudly at the next class meeting. Funny thing, though, my self-assessments didn't convince my tutor that I was doing as well as I thought. Teachers always know. It's as if they have eyes in the back of their heads, or a secret way of watching you at home while you give your readings. In my case, my teacher is a really good psychic and could see right through me. It was a good lesson in being honest in my self-assessments. It forced me to get serious with my analyses too: No more playing around. Playing around wouldn't help me to rise to the top.

The Tallies

In my mentorship training with Mavis, we looked at all aspects of being a medium, among them, bad habits. I had my fair share of bad habits to break. There were so many, I don't know where to begin, so I'll keep it simple and share only a few. As I've mentioned a few times (but it bears repeating!), when I gave a reading or did inspirational speaking, I had the habit of saying "Um"—a lot. Mavis (or Jean, Mavis' partner) would take a tally every time I said it. After the reading, they told me the ridiculous number of times I said "Um." I would take a deep breath, sigh, and wonder, "Why am I still doing this?" To this day, every time I catch myself saying "Um" while speaking publicly, I can see Jean tilting her head, looking at me out of the corners of her eyes, eyebrows slightly raised, with that lovely smile, saying, "You said Um thirty-six times, darling." I even find myself editing "Um" out of my YouTube videos. Yes, I confess, I still have "Um" issues. It is improving and one day I will master "Um." But whether it's a "throw-away word" like "Um" or "Uh," or "Ah," or it's another word we repeat often, we need to keep these filler words in check. Any word repeated often is both distracting to the audience and sounds unprofessional. What space-filler words makes your presentation less than perfect?

I am grateful to Jean and Mavis for helping me in countless ways with my presentations. For example, they made me aware of my tendency to stand in one spot while on platform, and how I would zoom in on my recipient, forgetting about the rest of the audience. Making eye contact with those who aren't receiving a message will draw them in, and they will listen even though the message isn't for them. If you zoom in on your recipient, it becomes more like a private sitting and you will lose your audience. So, I had to learn to stop my tunnel vision, make eye contact with the whole audience, engage with the audience, and use the entire platform (but not too much!). I remember once being asked to give an inspirational talk. I stepped to the front, was given my topic and, fully aware of my habit, I began. I walked back and forth across the platform the entire time. Jean, who was trying to videotape me, had trouble following me, and she and I had a nice laugh afterward at the thought of the video being blurry from Jean having to move it so much. Remember, when you walk across the platform, the audience will follow you with their eyes, and your movement will keep them engaged. But be careful not to make your audience dizzy!

I think "travelling the platform" was the easiest of all my bad habits to break. One of the harder habits to get a handle on was my annoying habit of frowning as I'm working. It's not a pretty frown, it's the frown a mother makes when she is about to scold her child. I discovered that I simply couldn't give a reading without frowning. If it weren't for Jean's videos, I would never have been aware of this not-so-pretty-face I made. I know you're wondering: "Did they keep a tally of every time Kay frowned?" The answer is "Yes, they did." Recently, I was on a week-long course with Mavis. It had been four years since I'd last seen Mavis and Jean. It was my turn to demonstrate in front of the class and unfortunately, Jean missed my demonstration. When Mavis told her how I did, Jean asked, "Did Kay make that face?" I'm proud to say that Mavis replied, "No, she didn't." Make forward progress, guys, that's all we can do! But can you see how mediumship encompasses far more than giving evidence? You have to be a good medium, a good public speaker, and exude confidence on the platform. It's a tall order, but if I can do it, you can too!

Checklists

In addition to keeping tally marks that helped us become aware of our annoying habits, my tutors also used checklists to analyze our work, checking repeated phrases, word choice, the structure of the reading, the number of times we paused, the type of evidence we gave, and which clairs we used, to just name a few. We would use these checklists to analyze our recordings as well. I liked using the checklists, they helped me to discover my not-so-good habits and to discern what I was doing well. Every time someone reminded me I was displaying a bad habit, it took me a step closer to conquering that habit for good. Let's face it, guys, most of the time when giving a reading, we are oblivious to those bad habits. The only way to move beyond them is to find out when they happen, and the only way to do that is by having trusted colleagues watch our work, checklist and pencil in hand. Of course, having someone point out your weaknesses is hard, but when you see the progress you are making, those checklists can make you feel wonderful too.

Discovering our strengths is always a warm-fuzzy, and we need all the warm-fuzzies we can get in this work.

Peer Analysis

I was comfortable with being analyzed by my tutors and eventually became comfortable analyzing myself. But analyzing my peers was awkward. As a beginner medium, who was I to evaluate someone whom I saw as far superior to me in their mediumship development? I didn't want to point out other's mistakes. My peers in the mentorship program had become life-long friends. I only wanted to point out the positive and make them feel fabulous. But I learned to move past these challenges by reminding myself that my critique was to help them grow, and that as my friend, I wanted them to improve. Sometimes the analysis wasn't done with a checklist, and instead, the third person in the group would watch the colors of the medium change as they worked. We would watch to see when spirit stepped in or out, to make sure the medium stayed in their power.

Our feedback to the medium during any reading was to be only "Yes," "No," "I don't know," or "I'm not sure." We could not add any other information. We could give feedback afterward but we kept it to a minimum because we knew we could bring the same communicator through on another day. Mediums are really good at reading between the lines and we are quick to give a "Yes" when we know what the medium giving the reading is talking about, even if they give vague evidence or get the evidence slightly wrong. But if we did this, the rules would have to change to the responses of "Yes" or "No" ... and for any evidence that was not 100% correct, we would have to say, "No." This meant the medium had to work extra hard to get the evidence correct.

Usually when we did this, we worked in a group of three mediums. One did the reading, one was the recipient, and the other did the analysis. This works well but only when the analyzer is honest with their feedback. There are ways to give a constructive critique in a gentle way, and as long as the medium knows it's coming, it should all go well. Think of it as a way to gently help your fellow mediums. As a developing medium, it is extremely helpful to have other mediums assess your work and I recommend that you incorporate checklists into your practice sessions and circles. And, if you ever move on to become a teacher of mediumship you'll need to analyze your peers, students, and yourself. You will also need to know how to read the aura, watch for when spirit steps in, and know when the medium has lost their power.

Growing as a Medium

Nobody likes doing self-assessments or being critiqued. But these are great tools to help us see what we are doing, recognize our strengths and weaknesses, and appreciate how much we have grown. "Growth" is the key word here. To rise to the top, we have to look at our work consistently and decide what our goals going forward will be.

I know how important it is to listen to and watch ourselves on video when we are in "learning mode" so we can see what everyone else sees. This is why I've suggested you record every mediumship reading you do. The day will come when you'll say to yourself, "I'm glad I recorded all these sessions and took the time to do reviews." You'll see how well you've nurtured the seeds you've planted.

To help you move more fully into your mediumship, it's also important to draw upon the strengths you already have in place. What skills have you learned up to this point in life that you can use to further your mediumship? For example, I use my teaching abilities all the time. As a teacher, I learned to deal with difficult situations, I learned to stay calm when everything around me felt like chaos, and I learned patience. The biggest strength from my teaching career was learning to speak in front of a large audience. I use all these skills in my mediumship every day.

Life is one huge lesson. The lessons along the way often help you with the lessons you are learning now. So, draw upon the strengths you've gained outside of mediumship to help you on this journey. Take your recordings seriously. Watch them. Look for your strengths. Look for one or two areas to focus on going forward. Celebrate any growth no matter how tiny. Remember, your recordings are a record of your journey, your growth. Look at them as your road to excellence.

Exercise 1

Private Sitting Reflection

Objective:

The objective of each exercise is to begin using assessments during your readings to gain a deeper understanding of your strengths and weaknesses.

Type of Reading:

I recommend doing all the readings as one-to-one sittings both psychically and mediumistically to get a good grasp on how to bring it all together. You may practice them in group or gallery settings using mediumistic faculties if you can get extra people or are working in a circle. One-to-one sittings are fifteen to thirty minutes long for the purpose of a practice exercise. Gallery style readings are seven to ten minutes long.

Materials Needed:

- Device to record your reading.
- Handouts for assessments:
  1. Private Sitting, Sitting Reflection Chart,
  2. Looking at Your Evidence Chart, and
  3. Psychic and Mediumship Reading Evaluation Chart.
- Journal.

Videos: (Optional)

1. Private Sitting, Sitting Reflection.
2. Looking at Your Evidence.

Number of Participants:

- Three works best, two minimum.

Extra Information:

- You have three exercises and three different charts to use. You can choose to do these all in one day or on separate days. If you choose to do them all on the same day, I recommend having one discussion about all three exercises at the end and one reflection in the journal. If you do the exercises on separate days, I recommend having a discussion and journal reflection on the same day, while your memory is fresh.

Table #21: Expectations: Exercise 1 – Private Sitting Reflection

Expectations: Exercise 1 Private Sitting Reflection		
Medium's Role	**Recipient's Role**	**Recorder's Role**
• Provide your sitter with an introduction to the reading.	• The sitter is the time keeper. Please let the medium know when they've exceeded their time.	• Using the Private Sitting Reflection form, record the evidence given under the appropriate category.
• Begin your reading. • Close your reading.	• Feedback should consist of "Yes," "No," "I don't know," or "I'm not sure." • No additional feedback is necessary.	• After the reading, discuss what you recorded with the medium and recipient.

Handout (Observer):

Table #22: Handout for Exercise 1 – (Observer) Private Sitting Reflection

Private Sitting Reflection (Observer)					
Introduction – Description of process and disclaimer (Please describe what was said, how the medium explained the process or what to expect, medium's demeanor, how long the reading lasted, how long it took to connect with spirit once intro was finished, etc.).	Evidence of Spirit Communicator Names, descriptions, memories, life experiences, etc. (Please List)	Evidence of Psychic Links Knowledge about the sitter – Health Job, Relationships, Finance, Uplifting message, etc. (Please List)	Deeper Evidence, Mind Journeys Descriptions of where someone lived (e.g. locality, house numbers, phone numbers), information about the home (e.g. description of home, what is in the cupboards or drawers), information about schools, churches, cars (e.g. make and model, license plate number). The Wow Factor (Write details)	Message or Words of Encouragement Did the medium offer the sitter any Advice/ Counseling, Encouragement? (Please describe)	Estimate a % of Accuracy (Based on all the evidenced received.)

Repeat this exercise as often as needed. It will help you, the medium, polish your delivery of evidence in your readings.

Handout (Sitter):

Table #23: Handout for Exercises 1, 2, and 3 – Sitter's Number of Spirit Communicators

---

Number of Spirit Communicators: _____

What general expressions did the medium use during the reading? Place a √ for each time a phrase is used.

Negative:
   I think _____ Do you know? _____ I'm not sure _____

   Can you place? _____ Let me go back _____ Ummm _____

   Waffling (repeating evidence, stalling) _____ Asked a question _____

Positive:
   I am aware _____ I know _____ I feel _____

   I see _____ I hear _____ They are telling me _____

Procedures:

1. Set your intent.
2. Hit "Record" on your phone or recorder.
3. Do the reading.
4. Stop recording.

Discussion with Group or Partner About the Process or Exercise:

1. How did it feel to evaluate your partners? Was it hard to mark them as less than perfect?
2. What value did you get from the process as the medium, recipient, and recorder?
3. Were there any Wow moments or gold nuggets?

4. Will you continue to use the forms to evaluate your progress?
5. What are your goals as you move forward?

Journal:

- Reflect on how you feel about your reading today. Write down your thoughts.
- Share any emotions or struggles that may have come up.
- What did you feel your strengths were? Where did you have challenges? Write these down.
- What was your gold nugget, the best bit of the reading?
- Close your eyes, take a few deep breaths, and ask your soul what wisdom it wants to leave with you today. Wait for it to come. Start writing.

Exercise 2

Looking at Your Evidence

Objective:

The objective of each exercise is to begin using assessments during your readings to gain a deeper understanding of your strengths and weaknesses.

Type of Reading:

I recommend doing all the readings as one-to-one sittings both psychically and mediumistically to get a good grasp on how to bring it all together. You may practice them in group or gallery settings using mediumistic faculties if you can get extra people or are working in a circle. One-to-one sittings are fifteen to thirty minutes long for the purpose of a practice exercise. Gallery style readings are seven to ten minutes long.

Materials Needed:

- Device to record your reading.
- Handouts for assessments:
    1. Private Sitting, Sitting Reflection Chart,
    2. Looking at Your Evidence Chart, and
    3. Psychic and Mediumship Reading Evaluation Chart.
- Journal.

Videos: (Optional)

1. Private Sitting, Sitting Reflection.
2. Looking at Your Evidence.

Number of Participants:

- Three works best, two minimum.

Extra Information:

- You have three exercises and three different charts to use. You can choose to do these all in one day or on separate days. If you choose to do them all on the same day, I recommend having one discussion about all three exercises at the end and one reflection in the journal. If you do the exercises on separate days, I recommend having a discussion and journal reflection on the same day, while your memory is fresh.

Table #24: Expectations: Exercise 2 – Looking at Your Evidence

Expectations: Exercise 2 Looking at Your Evidence		
Medium's Role	**Recipient's Role**	**Recorder's Role**
• Set your intention to connect with the name given to you. • Your goal is to bring through the evidence the sitter wrote down, even though you don't know what was written. • Provide your sitter with an introduction to the reading. • Begin your reading. • Close the reading.	• The sitter is the time keeper. Please let the medium know when they've exceeded their time. • Feedback should consist of "Yes," "No," "I don't know," or "I'm not sure." • No additional feedback is necessary	• Tell the medium whom you would like to have come through and their relationship to you. • Using the Looking at Your Evidence form, write down seven pieces of information you'd like to hear from the loved one you would like to have come through. • Record the evidence given under the appropriate category. • After the reading, discuss what you recorded with the medium and recipient.
It is possible that a different communicator will come through. That's okay, you will do this exercise many times.		

Handout:

Table #25: Handout for Exercise 2 – Looking at Your Evidence

	Looking at Your Evidence				
	Spirit Communicator's Name and Relationship to the Recipient _____ (Give name and relationship to medium before they begin the reading):				
	Write the seven pieces of evidence in rows 1-7 below before the reading begins. Fill in the evidence under the appropriate columns below.				
	Seven Pieces of Evidence that You, the Recipient, Would Like to Hear (Place a √ by each piece of evidence the medium gives. Do not share these seven pieces of evidence with the medium before the reading)	**Evidence that is Correct But Not Part of Seven Pieces Provided** (Not one of the seven listed)	**Misallocated Evidence** (Evidence is About Someone Else)	**Psychic Evidence** (Evidence is all about you, the sitter)	**Imagination** (You, the sitter, cannot take this evidence)
1					
2					
3					
4					
5					
6					
7					

Procedures:

1. Set your intent.
2. Hit "Record" on your phone or recorder.
3. Do the reading.
4. Stop recording.

Discussion with Group or Partner About the Process or Exercise:

1. How did it feel to evaluate your partners? Was it hard to mark them as less than perfect?
2. What value you did you get from the process as the medium, recipient, and recorder?
3. Were there any Wow moments or gold nuggets?
4. Will you continue to use the forms to evaluate your progress?
5. What are your goals as you move forward?

Journal:

- Reflect on how you feel about your reading today. Write down your thoughts.
- Share any emotions or struggles that may have come up.
- What did you feel your strengths were? Where did you have challenges? Write these down.
- What was your gold nugget, the best bit of the reading?
- Close your eyes, take a few deep breaths, and ask your soul what wisdom it wants to leave with you today. Wait for it to come. Start writing.

EXERCISE 3

Psychic & Mediumship Reading Evaluation

Objective:

The objective of each exercise is to begin using assessments during your readings to gain a deeper understanding of your strengths and weaknesses.

Type of Reading:

I recommend doing all the readings as one-to-one sittings both psychically and mediumistically to get a good grasp on how to bring it all together. You may practice them in group or gallery settings using mediumistic faculties if you can get extra people or are working in a circle. One-to-one sittings are fifteen to thirty minutes long for the purpose of a practice exercise. Gallery style readings are seven to ten minutes long.

Materials Needed:

- Device to record your reading.
- Handouts for assessments:
  1. Private Sitting, Sitting Reflection Chart,
  2. Looking at Your Evidence Chart, and
  3. Psychic and Mediumship Reading Evaluation Chart.
- Journal.

Videos: (Optional)

1. Private Sitting, Sitting Reflection.
2. Looking at Your Evidence.

Number of Participants:

- Three works best, two minimum.

Extra Information:

- You have three exercises and three different charts to use. You can choose to do these all in one day or on separate days. If you choose to do them all on the same day, I recommend having one discussion about all three exercises at the end and one reflection in the journal. If you do the exercises on separate days, I recommend having a discussion and journal reflection on the same day, while your memory is fresh.

Table #26: Expectations: Exercise 3 – Reading Evaluation

Expectations: Exercise 3 Reading Evaluation	
Medium's Role	**Recipient's Role**
• Provide your sitter with an introduction to the reading. • Begin your reading. • Close the reading.	• The sitter is the time keeper. Please let the medium know when they've exceeded their time. • Feedback should consist of "Yes," "No," "I don't know," or "I'm not sure." • No additional feedback is necessary. • Using the Reading Evaluation form, evaluate the reading. • After the reading, discuss with the medium what you recorded.

Handout:

Table #27: Expectations: Exercise 3 – Psychic and Mediumship
Private Reading Evaluation

	Psychic & Mediumship Private Reading Evaluation Please evaluate your medium honestly.	
1	Did the medium help you to feel at ease before beginning your session?	Yes No Somewhat
2	Did the medium identify your loved one(s) accurately, leaving no doubt as to whom the medium was communicating with?	Yes No Somewhat
3	Did the medium provide evidence of your loved one's life in details? Example: personality, where they lived, hobbies, career, relationship to you, how they passed.	Yes No Somewhat
4	Did the medium go beyond generic evidence? Generic evidence examples: hair, height, loves you, clothing, etc.	Yes No Somewhat
5	Did the medium provide names or significant dates around you or your loved one?	Yes No Somewhat
6	Did the medium provide a specific memory unique to you and your loved one?	Yes No Somewhat
7	Did the medium deliver a message from your loved one, leaving you feeling uplifted or encouraged?	Yes No Somewhat
8	Did the medium attempt a psychic connection? Did they inform you that it was coming from their psychic faculty?	Yes No Somewhat
9	Did the medium ask if you had any questions at the end of the reading?	Yes No
10	How would you rate your overall experience with this reading?	Excellent Fair Needed More
11	Would you pay for this reading if the medium were a working medium?	Yes No Not sure
12	Would you recommend this medium to a friend or family member?	Yes No Maybe

Procedures:

1. Set your intent.
2. Hit "Record" on your phone or recorder.
3. Do the reading.
4. Stop recording.

Discussion with Group or Partner About the Process or Exercise:

1. How did it feel to evaluate your partners? Was it hard to mark them as less than perfect?
2. What value you did you get from the process as the medium, recipient, and recorder?
3. Were there any Wow moments or gold nuggets?
4. Will you continue to use the forms to evaluate your progress?
5. What are your goals as you move forward?

Journal:

- Reflect on how you feel about your reading today. Write down your thoughts.
- Share any emotions or struggles that may have come up.
- What did you feel your strengths were? Where did you have challenges? Write these down.
- What was your gold nugget, the best bit of the reading?
- Close your eyes, take a few deep breaths, and ask your soul what wisdom it wants to leave with you today. Wait for it to come. Start writing.

*What you do makes a difference
and you have to decide what kind of difference
you want to make.*

—Jane Goodall

Chapter 11

"Ethics"

With mediumship, you never know what will happen. When you begin to work, you never know what you're going to get or who will show up. Surprises greet you at every turn. So, as a professional medium, you have to be prepared to handle the unexpected. Not all Spirit Communicators lived happy, healthy, honorable lives here on earth, and this chapter covers what to do when you encounter a challenging link. Perhaps your spirit communicator was abusive or unkind in life or perhaps they suffered from mental illness or addiction—we'll address how to handle those links. Similarly, not all your recipients will be hale and hearty ... so we'll also cover what to do when your recipient needs help or professional care.

Psychometry Reading

Early in my mediumship development, I met a gentleman named Bob at my local mediumship circle who came to my house for a free reading. I invited him in, offered him a cup of tea, and we chatted for a few minutes before getting started. He wanted a mediumship reading which was great because I could feel the spirit world coming close. I brought through several family members, the reading went well, and at the end, I asked, "Do you have any questions?"

He asked, "Would you be willing to use psychometry on a photo I have?"

I nodded.

He handed me an envelope containing the photo. I didn't ask him anything about the photo, I just held the envelope in one hand and placed my other hand on top. As I began feeling into the contents of the envelope I knew immediately it was a photo of a man. I gave evidence of his personality.

Bob said "Yes" to everything I gave him.

Suddenly, the evidence began to change. I felt as if I was in a dark, whirling hole of nothingness, spinning out of control. I felt deep sadness and loneliness. The more my world spun, the deeper into darkness I fell.

Bob was saying, "Yes, yes, yes," so I continued.

"The person in the picture felt trapped and often didn't know how to move forward," I said. "He was intelligent but these bouts of darkness were too much for him to bear on his own. Yet, he didn't know how to get help."

My sitter said "Yes" to all the evidence.

Suddenly I realized that the person I was describing was sitting across from me in my living room. I stopped, looked at him and said, "This is you."

He smiled. "Yes," he said. "You described my entire life. You were spot on."

I sat there, speechless. I knew he was different than most people, and spent a great deal of time alone·or with his mother (even though he was in his fifties). But I'd had no idea he suffered in this way.

We chatted for a little while about him getting help.

Bob continued, "I had tried many times but couldn't afford to go to a psychologist or psychiatrist."

"That must have been difficult for you," I replied.

"Yes," said Bob, "I have lived on disability my whole adult life which makes it hard for me to keep a job. When the darkness comes, I don't leave the house for weeks at a time."

This was the first reading I had ever done where my recipient was struggling with depression or mental illness. I wasn't sure how to handle the situation. I drew upon my experiences working in the school system. For example, sometimes a parent would come in for a conference with visible bruises on her body. Other times it became obvious through a parent-teacher conversation that home was not a safe environment. On these occasions, my compassion and empathy kicked into high gear and I applied some of the coaching techniques that all teachers know. So, with Bob, I used my coaching know-how, and urged him to seek professional help. It was all I knew to do.

He had been at my house for over an hour. To hurry him out the door, I told him I had another appointment. I knew if I didn't usher him out, he would have stayed another hour. We said our goodbyes and he thanked me for the free reading. I closed the door, walked into the living room, and stood there in disbelief. I was overwhelmed and mentally and physically exhausted.

About an hour later, I heard a knock at the door. I peeked outside; it was Bob returning. He was holding something. I couldn't bring myself to answer the door so I watched through the window as he got back into his car and drove away. I noticed that whatever he'd been holding was no longer in his hands. That struck me as odd so I went downstairs and opened the front door. There on the steps was a bag from our local supermarket. Inside there were fresh blueberries and a note. I can't remember his exact words, but the note went something like, "Thank you for offering to a do a free reading for me. I can't afford to give you any money but I saw these blueberries and thought you might like them. Thank you for taking extra time to talk to me." I felt horrible for not opening the door for him. After reading his note and seeing his kind gesture, I felt even worse.

Not a Counselor

I was completely unprepared to help Bob. As noted, at the time I was not a working medium. This session served as a lesson to me about the many types of people who will cross our paths. I realized right then that in order to help Bob I would have needed more information—information that I got eventually, and that I want to share with you now. The issues I'll cover are not in any order of importance, but each of them may arise for you.

If you are an empath, be careful and make sure you take care of *you* first. In my case, my empathy for others got to me when I refused to open the door when Bob came back to my house. Remember, our role is not as counselor to our clients. I knew that if Bob had stepped back into my house, I'd find myself in an uncomfortable position, sitting across from someone who wanted me to put on a counselor's hat. It was what he needed and he felt comfortable talking to me. But I'm not a trained therapist—and unless we have a counseling degree, the best we can do for a client like this is to refer them to a counselor or agency that can help them. That said, even if I were trained in psychoanalysis, I would still refer my mediumship clients to someone else, because I wouldn't want to blur the lines between "counselor" and "medium." In my opinion, those two roles should remain separate.

Recipients in Need

Over the years, I've learned that we as mediums will have clients coming to us who need many different kinds of professional help. And some people seek out a psychic or medium hoping to find that help. Sometimes during a spirit communication, you may realize that your recipient suffered abuse at the hands of the spirit communicator, or the spirit communicator may lead you to the knowledge that your client is in an abusive situation and needs help. In the case of Bob (the gentleman who came to my house), I knew intuitively to stop the reading once I realized he was the person I was reading. At any time you feel your client is not mentally stable, the best thing to do is stop the reading. It will be handy to keep some business cards or brochures for professional counselors, psychologists, or mental health agencies in a drawer in your office.

Then, when you find yourself in a situation where it's not the right time for a client to be having a mediumship reading, you can say simply, "I don't think now is the right time for you to have this reading. I'm going to stop the reading now and refund your money." Then, hand them a business card or pamphlet on where they can go for help. Be compassionate, show empathy, and explain that the professionals you are referring them to are better options for them at this time.

The protocol would be similar for those suffering from substance abuse or narcotic abuse. As long as a sitter is straight and sober when they arrive for the reading, it's fine to proceed with the reading. But if you smell alcohol on their breath or you know your client is tipsy, I wouldn't give them a reading.

As noted, sometimes in a reading you may discover that your client is in an abusive situation. As long as the client is okay emotionally at the time of the session, I would continue the reading. Using my psychic faculties, I may see ways she (or he) could lessen the tensions at home. Again, I would not counsel such a client in the manner a therapist would, but I might recommend places they could go for safety or suggest people in their life who could help.

For survivors of abuse, be mindful of word choices during a reading—be respectful and gentle. I'm also mindful of spirit communicators who abused the sitter—sometimes the recipient is not ready to hear from the abuser. I honor that; I tell the spirit communicator the recipient isn't ready to hear from them, thank them for coming through, and send them on their way.

No matter what the situation is, have promotional materials on hand so you can point your client toward professional help.

Spirit Communicators

I've had several spirit communicators come through in readings who were less than kind in life, some were even abusers. As mediums, we have to make quick decisions on how to handle such situations. As noted earlier, word choice as well as empathy and compassion become important—for both those in the unseen world and for the recipient.

In a public demonstration once, I had a spirit communicator, a friend of the recipient, who portrayed herself as kind, a bit shy, but a nice person to be around. She showed me her work place, her social life, and a few memories of having outings with her friend. The more I worked my recipient's loved one, the more I began to feel a shift in her energy. It was as if everything I'd said about her personality was no longer true. This puzzled me. I wasn't sure how to show what I was now feeling. Choosing my words carefully I said, "You would understand that your friend had two sides to her personality."

"Yes," said the recipient.

I continued, saying, "I'm aware that she often battled with these two sides. At times, it became too much for her to handle."

"Yes," the recipient said.

"She's showing me that her friends," I said, "including you, would often try to help her. But your efforts were not enough. She wants you all to know how grateful she is for all you did to help her."

The recipient nodded.

I continued, saying, "She's making me aware of her passing. She says, "I'm sorry. I didn't mean to hurt anyone."

The recipient nodded again. A tear rolled down her cheek.

At that point, I knew the spirit communicator had said what she needed to say ... and the recipient had heard what she needed to hear. I brought the contact to a close. There was no need to describe this woman's passing. I was in a public setting, so I limited the personal information and instead chose my words carefully, getting the point across so the recipient would know what I was seeing and what the communicator was revealing.

As you can see, the delivery of the evidence we receive is as important as the evidence itself.

Be mindful of your words and the impact those words will have on your recipient. Be mindful too of revealing too much in a public presentation. A skilled medium knows how to choose words that soften the evidence. We are not changing the evidence, we are delivering it in a way that will not trigger trauma for the recipient. By not revealing to the audience more than they need to know, we are respecting our recipient.

It happens often that spirit communicators portray themselves to me one way at first, and then as we move deeper into the reading and they show me a different life setting (usually their home life), they are the complete opposite. Early in my training, for example, I had a dad come through for his son. I was at the College and we were working in small groups. The dad portrayed himself as a professional, driven to do well at work, and a jolly man in the pubs with his friends. He was well-liked in the professional world and people would rely on him for direction or help in the field.

His son looked at me, shook his head and said, "No, that's not Dad."

I made my famous frown-face, I'm sure, and delved back into the evidence to see how I could word the evidence in a way he would understand. I saw a flash of darkness, then two images of his dad side by side, with a dark line separating them. I thought "This is odd." I felt deeper into the image and felt two personas with this father. I said to the son, "Your dad is showing me that his personality at home was different from his personality when he was away from home. He makes me aware of people always walking on eggshells at home so as not to upset him. He also makes me aware of a lot of fear felt at home."

"Yes, that is correct," the recipient said.

I didn't want to get too personal as there were others listening. I ended the reading by noting that people outside their home saw the father in a different way than his family saw him. The son said, "Yes, that makes sense." He added, "I knew him at home and at home he was a monster."

This reading was the first time a communicator with two distinct personalities had come through. Any time something new occurs in a reading, I make a mental note afterward about what the energy felt like when I received the evidence. This way when it happens again I will remember the feeling and be able to deliver the evidence correctly.

The next time a similar communicator came through, I recognized the energy. I also saw the flash of darkness, which confirmed to me that I could have someone with two different personalities. As I became more aware of these types of communicators, I no longer had the flash of darkness. I could feel the subtle change in energy.

When I say that some communicators I've brought through have had "two different personalities," I am not inferring that they had a mental illness like dissociative identity disorder (split personality), though some may have been mentally ill. I'm simply saying that in one setting their behavior or personality was different from the way they were in another setting. We all know people, for example, whose personality is outgoing and fun around those they are close to but when they are around strangers, they become shy. With practice, mediums can learn to feel the subtle change in energy, whether you are dealing with someone with mental illness or just someone who moves between extroversion and introversion depending on what environment they are in.

A Medium's Responsibilities

Being a medium is multi-faceted. We wear many hats and master many skills. When I began my mediumship journey, I thought I just needed to learn to connect and bring through strong evidence so the recipient would know who had come to speak to them. I laugh now at my naivete. To be a medium, we must package evidence artfully. We must be word mavens; we must be kind, compassionate, and empathic. We must also be great actors—we have to know to read body language and facial cues, and must respond in a heartbeat to nuances in our sitter's responses—and so much more. Here's a bit more detail on two very important abilities we as mediums must become experts in:

o   Become a wordsmith: I've already mentioned that as mediums we have to choose our words wisely. If there is anything I impress upon you, I hope this is it. There is much truth in the phrase, "*Words matter.*" What do I mean when I say this? Here are some of the red flags and circumstances that cue me to pay extra attention to my words. I may become aware of:

- substance abuse
- abuse has occurred or the abuser has come through
- trauma
- traumatic passing
- suicide
- emotions
- body cues which suggest the sitter is uncomfortable
- when a passing is still fresh for the sitter, and they feel emotionally raw, or
- when a child in spirit comes through.

In all these situations, I take extra care to use appropriate and sensitive language. Similarly, when a reading takes place in a public forum, I exercise caution in this area as well.

o   Learn to Read Body Language: We need always to be aware of our recipient, their reactions, and their emotional or mental state when their loved ones come through. They will often send signals with their body movements or we may pick up emotions on a psychic level. We do sacred work, so always use compassion and empathy. Both of these emotions are essential in the work of a medium. But there's a slight but distinct difference between compassion and empathy: *Compassion* is being sympathetic of others with a desire to help them. *Empathy* is the ability to relate to the pain of another person as if we have experienced the pain ourselves—we experience the feelings of others vicariously. So, during any reading, if you feel at any time (and for any reason) that the reading needs to end, it's okay to end it. Your compassion and your empathy will tell you what is right in any given situation.

Children in the Spirit World

Children who have passed to the spirit world love to come and visit family members. It's been my experience that if a communicator is very young, they will come with an adult in spirit to help with the communication. I've never had a baby communicate with me but I have been aware of an adult in the spirit world coming to let the recipient know that they have the baby with them and all is well.

When we are communicating with a sitter's child in spirit, obviously compassion and empathy for the recipient are necessary. I always give evidence of their personality and then allow the spirit child to lead the way if they are able to do so. Often, I find they want to talk about the happy moments and want their parents to know they are still around them, and love them dearly. Equally as often, they come to tell mommy and daddy not to be so sad and they let them know how wonderful their life in the unseen world is.

I keep it simple when a child comes through, for it can be too much for a parent to relive their child's passing. Knowing that their child made it to the spirit world, that loved ones are watching over the little one, and that they are still around is all they need to know.

Once when I was giving a demonstration with a friend, right away I became aware of a baby or toddler in the spirit world. This little girl was with me the entire night. On my very last contact, I mentioned her and described the grandmother who was with the child. I went to a woman on the front row who looked to be in her eighties. "Do you know this child?" I asked.

"Yes," she said.

I said, "She was your little girl." She burst into tears. "Yes," she said.

This shows you that it does not matter how many years have passed since you last held your child. The love and pain are still there. This woman had waited years for her baby girl to come speak to her. The little girl wanted her mum to know she was there. The grandmother was the spirit communicator but the message was delivered.

Lead with Compassion

Our world is ever-changing and we must move with the change. Unfortunately, these changes often involve trauma, abuse, addiction, suicide, mental illness, and more. They show up in both clients and spirit communicators, so we must consistently practice compassion and empathy in our work as mediums. Similarly, it's important that we be ever mindful of our sitters' emotions and body language, as well as our own. This is especially important when you have a traumatic situation unfolding. For example, if you have a spirit communicator who committed suicide, you would craft your words carefully. You wouldn't blurt out "He committed suicide" in a matter-of-fact way, instead you would deliver the evidence softly, using words such as "I feel he was responsible for his own passing."

I am very careful with a communicator who completed suicide. I wait until the evidence has come three times to make sure I am receiving it correctly. I don't want to take any chances on being wrong with such a serious manner of passing. For example, I might begin with, "I know your uncle had great difficulty controlling his emotions. I'm aware that he often secluded himself, staying away from those who love him for long periods. He makes me aware of several times he had thoughts of leaving this world. I know he deeply regrets what he put his family through. He comes today to ask for forgiveness."

In doing it this way, you're leading up to the reason he passed, and softening the evidence. This way, you may not have to say "suicide" or "He took his own life." The recipient knows exactly where you are going. Another way to soften it would be to say "I feel your uncle had a part in his passing." You aren't saying "suicide," which can feel cold. Imagine how difficult it would be for a parent to hear a medium blurt out, without compassion,

"Your son committed suicide." It must feel like a jolt of lightning going through them.

Whenever an abuse or trauma survivor comes through, or whenever someone who has difficult life experiences or mental challenges steps forward to engage with their loved one here in the physical world, it opens the door for healing to take place in our world and in the unseen world. How wonderful it is when we see a beautiful exchange of forgiveness or the first steps on the road to healing.

Finally, as a reading unfolds, we must be aware of and sensitive to the emotional, physical, and mental states of our recipient. For example, we would not want to continue if we see that the sitter is experiencing any distress or discomfort. Again, having referral material such as business cards on hand can make all the difference in helping your client find the help they need.

EXERCISE 1

Resources for Clients

In this exercise, you are going to envision creating a space and resources with which you can help any client that may need assistance beyond the mediumship services you offer.

Make a list of professional agencies that can help with the issues noted below. Collect business cards and brochures for therapists, psychologists, and other professionals. Give your client a pamphlet from each respective agency. If the client's home is not a safe place for them, keep information on hand for telephone help lines, halfway houses, triage centers, and women's and children's shelters. Check with your local mental health center to see if they have information you can give to clients as well. Here are some ideas about helping organizations you may wish to keep referral information on:

- Addiction
- Grief
- Trauma
- Abuse.

o Create a list of hotline numbers such as:
  - National Domestic Violence
  - Pathways to Safety International
  - Gay, Lesbian, Bisexual, and Transgender National Hotline
  - Sexual Assault – Rape, Abuse, Incest Hotlines
  - National Suicide Prevention Lifeline

- National Alliance on Mental Illness Helpline
- Substance Abuse and Mental Health Services Helpline.

○ Have a list of support groups on hand:
  - Grief support
  - Support groups for parents who have lost a child
  - Trauma support
  - Al-Anon
  - Alcoholics Anonymous.

Journal:

- Reflect on how you feel about today's assignment. Write your thoughts down.
- Share any emotions or struggles that may have come up.
- Close your eyes, take a few deep breaths, and ask your soul what wisdom it wants to leave with you today. Wait for it to come. Start writing.

From a tiny acorn, a mighty oak will grow.

CHAPTER 12

"THE PROFESSIONAL MEDIUM"

How do you know if you are ready to become a professional medium? It's the million-dollar question and it weighs heavily on the minds of many who follow this path. Perhaps you've asked everyone you know—and received a different answer from each person! Sorting through the varying viewpoints is daunting. But you've done the work faithfully, you've covered all of the exercises in this book, and you know you're getting close.

We know it takes time—many years of dedication and consistent practice in fact—to master the mediumship craft and to create a well-stocked tool box for the spirit world to work with. So, how do you know when you're ready to embrace the world of the professional, working medium? It's easy to say that "One must follow their inner voice when making this decision," but it's true, you should listen to your inner voice.

You know that being a medium involves much more than the mechanics of conducting a reading, and much more than connecting with those who have passed to the other side. It's more than relaying evidence of loved ones' survival in the spirit world and more than passing on messages of love. Mediums also serve as healers for those left behind as well as for those who have passed. We are the bridge that brings the two worlds together, allowing healing to take place, and with that role comes many responsibilities. Before "going professional," take a look at where you are in your development with regard to:

- the mechanics of mediumship,
- your general understanding of the spirit world, and
- how you package your evidence with empathy and compassion.

Have you mastered these criteria? As you reflect on your development, ask yourself the following questions. "Yes" answers to each of these questions will establish that you have met the prerequisites for "going professional."

o Does my evidence flow smoothly from my spirit communicator, through me to my client?

o Can I can hold my power for the length of the reading?

o When a client says "No" to a piece of evidence, do I continue without allowing the "No" to stop me? Do I stay in my power?

o Have I mastered the art of delivering evidence in a way that I am not triggering potential trauma for the recipient? Do I understand the ethics of mediumship and the power of words? Do I show empathy and compassion to everyone involved—on both sides of the veil?

o Do I have information, links, phone numbers, and business cards of agencies to share with my client if they need a consultation with a doctor, counselor, or other professional means of support?

o Has my training given me a strong understanding of the spirit world? Can I answer tough questions my client might ask during a reading? For example, what would my answer be if my client asked me:

- "What happens when we die?"
- "Who is taking care of my baby in the spirit world?"
- "Do children in the spirit world grow up?"
- "Is my friend who is responsible for taking their own life okay now?"

- "Why can't I feel my loved one like I did when they first passed?"

Here are three things you can do to determine whether or not you meet the standards expected of a professional medium:

- Create a simple checklist. You can even add a few extra items to your list. Think of your strengths, write them down. Now add the weaknesses—how are you doing with them?
- Ask your recipient or sitter for permission to voice-record their reading. Explain that you are using their reading to assess your own development.
- After each reading, listen to the recording. Make notes on your checklist, and review the results. Be honest.

Many mediums ease their way into charging clients. If you are not quite ready to charge a full per-session rate, consider the following options:

- Practice giving full readings on people you've never given a reading to. Ask for an honest opinion on the value of the reading. Give them your checklist, and have them evaluate you.
- Be up front with your recipients. Tell them what you are doing and why. It's okay to suggest to them that they can tip you or make a donation if they are happy with the reading.
- If you are almost ready to be a full-time professional, research the going rate for a medium in your area. Charge half that price until you feel you are ready to charge full price.

My First Platform Demonstration

I will never forget my first platform demonstration. I was a new medium about six or seven months into my first circle. The circle tutors were confident I was ready to make an attempt at doing a platform demonstration, and the tutor arranged for a presentation in our local home for the elderly. If memory serves, there were four of us working that night.

I started my reading beautifully. An entire family came to speak to a woman in the audience—it was as if a family reunion was taking place in the spirit world, with so many loved ones coming through, keeping up was overwhelming. I carried on anyway, I was so naïve I didn't realize what a hard task it was to work with so many communicators at one time. I gave wonderful evidence of family gatherings and memories. I don't remember getting "No's" from the recipient. However, just as I was getting in the groove, I froze. The color drained from my face. I turned and looked at my tutors without saying a word. I don't know what they saw when they looked at me but one of them jumped up and came to my rescue. She placed her hand on my back, reassuring me. She finished the reading. I was so embarrassed. I had never had that happen. I lowered my head and walked back to my seat. I sat there the rest of the evening wondering, "What happened?"

As we were leaving the venue, the tutor asked me, "What happened up there?" I shook my head. "I have no idea. I froze. I couldn't continue."

She said the look on my face was pure fear. Both circle leaders were concerned I would never want to do platform again after that night.

"I'm not going to let one night of terror stand in my way," I said.

I continued on in that circle, knowing I wasn't ready for the platform, knowing I needed to develop as a medium before returning. I continued sitting in the power daily and practicing on my friends every chance I could. When the time was right, I tried again. It was better.

Mediums are always eager to get out into public and work. We are guilty of taking one or two classes and thinking, "I'm good to go." The reality is that never happens. There are natural mediums who make contact easily with the spirit world with little training but a professional, well-polished medium takes guidance from someone who is knowledgeable and has walked the walk. They demonstrate patience and allow their development the time needed to become a professional.

The Confident Medium

I could write an entire book about my struggle to become confident about my mediumship. Finally, after all these years, I can say, "I am a confident medium." However, one bad reading or one-off night in public can send me spiraling backward. The struggle is real. I've learned to shrug it off and not let it bog me down for days as I did before. Now I know there is every reason to believe that my next contact will be fabulous.

You know you have confidence when you can stand up in front of an audience without notice and make a contact. There's no freaking out because you haven't prepared. You walk to the platform, head held high. You step into your power and begin.

I was giving a talk one night to a group of people about my spiritual journey, my background, and my life. At the end of the talk, someone asked about my mediumship: "How do you work?" I began to explain but realized it would be easier to show them. I gave instructions on what to do if I came to them, stepped into my power, and began working. That's confident mediumship—and if you're not there yet, don't worry. You will be.

Body language is another indicator of confidence—head held high, shoulders back, you command the platform or the sitting. There's no wavering. There's no "Um's" and no "I think's" coming out of your mouth. Everything about you says, "I know what I'm doing and this is going to be wonderful." You're the leader. Everyone knows you are in charge. You trust in the spirit world completely. You trust in yourself as a medium. You know what you're doing, you trust the evidence, you deliver. You don't doubt anything, and you trust the spirit world before you believe the recipient or the audience. The spirit world always gets it right. The recipient might have difficulty remembering on the spot—they'll remember after they've walked away. Be proud of who you are and exude confidence. I know you can do it!

The Polished Medium

A working medium is a polished medium. But what does that mean? To me, a polished medium delivers evidence smoothly, with few pauses, and if they do pause, it's only for a few seconds. They are masters of word choice and they know how to package evidence professionally to deliver it to the recipient. The polished medium brings their spirit communicator to life by allowing the communicator to tell their story. They deliver evidence in story form so the entire audience can follow along. They have learned how to work the energy of the room while on the platform. They can feel when the energy in the room begins to drop and they create laughter to raise the energy. They may finish a contact and pause for a moment to chat casually with the audience in order to re-engage them. They are mindful of how important the audience is to the demonstration. They also try to work with audience members all over the audience: back row, middle row, left, right, in the front. They throw their energy all the way to the back, they cover the entire space. If you watch a lot of demonstrations, you'll note that less experienced mediums may go to the front rows only, their energy isn't strong enough (yet) to reach the back. They still have work to do. But the polished medium can expand their energy and encircle the room. Does this sound like you? If yes, well done. Your hard work is coming into fruition. If this isn't you, no worries. It only means you need to keep nourishing the treasures within. You can and will get here!

The Whole Medium

My training consisted of training "the whole medium." The whole medium moves beyond giving a reading. As whole mediums, we are inspirational speakers, we work from the soul, we honor the sacredness of the work, and we understand the plight of pioneers who paved the way for us today. As inspired speakers, we know how to stand up and speak without preparation. We allow our souls to rise and speak on a topic our audience will resonate with or on a topic the audience needs to hear about. Using our intuition and our soul, we make a split-second decision—and begin.

When I do inspirational speaking, often I begin with a little introduction, saying something funny, making the audience laugh and bringing the energy up in the room. By the time I'm done with my chat, my soul and I are ready to work. I often lose myself in the talk and forget half of what I have said. At the end, I always ask someone, "Did it all make sense? Did it all flow?" I always get great feedback. That's the whole, confident medium at work. You trust, you surrender, and you know that your soul and the spirit world are working in tandem.

Are you wondering why it is important for mediums to learn to do inspired speaking? For a long time, I thought, "When I'm a professional, I'm never going to need this." I saw inspired speaking in the same way I saw algebra: "I'll never use this in the real world." I couldn't have been more wrong (about the inspired speaking, but not about the algebra). As a working medium, especially in America where inspired speaking isn't widely accepted (yet), I see great value in giving an inspired talk to platform audiences. Perhaps, for example, you feel the need intuitively to speak on an aspect of spirituality, the afterlife, or any topic the audience's souls need. There is nothing stopping you from giving a ten- to fifteen-minute talk through inspiration. The more I work, the more I realize the deep hunger for the general audience's desire for spiritual understanding. Who better to give that talk than a medium? Are you ready to step up to the challenge and give an inspired speaking presentation?

I prefer inspired speaking over giving a talk with PowerPoint or notes. In my opinion, when you allow the soul to rise and speak, you are speaking directly to the souls of those listening.

You touch their souls, your auric field emanates throughout the room, and the audience feels it. It is a beautiful spiritual moment for all. With notes or a PowerPoint deck on the other hand, you are speaking only to the audience's mind. They will not feel your aura—so the chances of you touching their souls is not great. Of course, there is a time and place for PowerPoint presentations and for speaking from notes. But a mediumship platform demonstration is a spiritual event, and lends itself to inspirational speaking.

The whole medium understands the importance of honoring the soul. As mediums, our soul does the majority of the work— Yes, even when we are giving a reading. So, it is important to form a relationship with our soul. This is why I had you write the soul letters. I hope you continue writing to your soul and that you allow your soul to write back. It will also help you with your inspirational speaking.

The Sacredness of Our Work

It is said that "You cannot be anywhere God is not." The Divine spark of the Creator (of your choosing) resides within all. Therefore, He is always a part of all we do. Understanding the sacredness of the work we do is another aspect of developing the craft of "the whole medium." As I mentioned in the beginning, Gordon Higginson's quote "Before you can touch the Spirit, you must find it within yourself for all truth, all knowledge and all loving must first be found within oneself." I never understood fully what this meant (or how it related to mediums). Now that I do understand, I find my mindset shifting and my soul rising. I'm sure it will shift again as that is what happens when you are searching continuously for truth. But I believe that our spirit and soul reside in the core of our being. I know that all our work as mediums moves first through the solar plexus—the center of our physical energy system—and I believe the Divine spark connecting us to our Creator runs through the solar plexus as well.

Mediums need to believe in a higher consciousness because we work through this Divine consciousness—we can't work effectively without touching the higher consciousness or "Spirit within." When we sit in the power we are expanding the power of that Divine spark and connecting to the Creator. We know that the stronger our power, the stronger the connection to our spirit communicator. Once we touch the spirit within, we will find the higher power, the God source. Sitting in the power is one way to touch Spirit. Prayer is another way.

I'm not saying that because we are mediums, we need to go to church. Many of us do not belong to a traditional church—some choose spiritual centers or do not belong to a congregation at all. It doesn't matter, as long as you understand the connection mediums have with a higher power and how the higher power assists us in our work.

Remember I told you that when I was around twelve years old, I asked my mom, "Why do dead people come to me in my dreams to deliver messages for you?" I didn't know these people so why were they coming to me? Why would I wake up knowing I had to relay a message to Mom that made no sense to me at all?

Recall too that Mom gave me the best response. "God needs messengers on Earth to help Him reach people here. He uses these messengers to deliver messages from Heaven. You can feel honored that God has asked you to help Him do His work."

As a twelve-year-old kid, that was all the explanation I needed; it made perfect sense. Of course God needs messengers on Earth—and who better to do that than a medium who has learned to move between the two worlds? As whole mediums, we acknowledge that we are messengers for higher consciousness, we are a channel for the spirit world, and we are a voice for the voiceless. We honor that sacredness in our work.

The Pioneers

Throughout my training, I heard stories about the amazing work our mediumship pioneers did in paving an easier path for mediums today. Life was not easy for them. The general public feared mediums, and throughout history being burned at the stake, being thrown in jail, and being publicly ridiculed were commonplace occurrences. Those brave women and men paved the way for us to be able to do our work relatively freely today—of course there are still those who think we are a bit batty, but at least they will not have the authorities cart us off to the loony bin.

One of the last mediums imprisoned in the United Kingdom was the great trance medium Helen Duncan. Among her many amazing mediumship skills, Mrs. Duncan produced ectoplasm. Fearing she might betray the country by giving away wartime secrets during her seances, the authorities sentenced her to nine months in jail. She served that time, and when released, she continued her work. She was arrested again for conducting a séance but was later released. About six days later, she passed to the spirit world. (Like Helen Duncan, many of other mediumship pioneers did wonderful trance work, much of which was written down and published. Maurice Barbanell, for example, a British journalist, was a well-known medium who allowed a guide by the name of "Silver Birch" to speak through him. I read his *Silver Birch* books often. He talks about the spirit world, our world, and he answers many questions posed by members of Maurice Barbanell's circle group. You can find the *Silver Birch* books on Amazon in print and Kindle versions.)

So, remember, when things get challenging with your mediumship, keep things in perspective. Not that long ago, people were thrown into prison just for being mediums. In Helen Duncan's case, over sixty years later, her granddaughter is still fighting to have her conviction overturned. I recommend that you learn about our pioneers, the work they did, and the unbearable hardships they tolerated in order to practice their craft. As noted, it is because of their selfless hard work and dedication that we are able to work with relatively little negative backlash (compared to what they endured). Even today, many mediums work undercover because they know their family and friends will not understand what they do. The day is coming, however, when the public as a whole will accept mediums and the valuable work we do. Just remember, you are following in the footsteps of the great pioneers. Stand tall and allow your light to shine— just as they did!

Seekers of Truth

Professional mediums are always searching for ways to improve their craft. For us, this is a life-long journey of learning and trying new ways of working. Professional mediums are truth-seekers, we all question what we see and hear. We nurture all aspects of ourselves, the psychical, the mental, and the spiritual. We balance our mediumship with readings and inspired speaking, we work from the soul, and we honor the blessed work we do. When we work, we make it look effortless.

Professional mediums serve as messengers for the spirit world. We are the bridge between two worlds, and both worlds need us. My hope is that we will all work from a place of truth and integrity always, so that we can serve both the spirit world and the physical world and enrich, empower, and enlighten the lives of others.

Embrace the spiritual treasures hidden within your soul. Nurture yourself emotionally, physically, and spiritually. Touch the God source within. Seek your truths not on the outside but on the inside—for that is where all the wisdom resides. You have all you need buried deep within your soul. Your destiny is set. You hold the key to unlock your full potential and set your soul free. So, get on with it. Your soul is ready to rise!

                                                     — ᘒ —

Exercise 1

Create a Plan to Move Forward on Your Spiritual Journey

Objective 1:

Reflect on your strengths as medium. What would you like to improve? Create a plan—how will you manifest your desires?

Instructions for Exercise 1:

1. Create a chart similar to the example below.
2. Reflect on your mediumship. What do you feel are your strengths? Where have you had success? Write them under the label called "Strengths and Success."
3. Think of the treasure chest brimming with precious jewels that you are creating for the spirit world. What do you really want to see added to that treasure chest over the next year? Make a list. Now choose three items and prioritize them. Write them under the label labeled "Desires."
4. Write an affirmation for each of your desires. I like to begin with "I am," because it implies "I am already doing this." You may have another way of writing your affirmations, and that's fine. Just keep them simple and to the point. For, me it's easier for my forgetful brain to remember if it's simple.

5. For the coming year, meditate on your mantra; visualize yourself already doing the thing you are affirming.

6. I made a photo collage on my computer and added my mantras, then made this collage my background screen. Every morning when I turn my computer on, I see my mantras. As I say the mantras, I visualize each one as already happening.

Here is an example:

Table #28: Strength and Success, Desires, Affirmation, Manifest

Strength and Success	Desires	Affirmation	Manifest
• I conquered my bad habit of saying "Um" after every other word. • I can do a mind journey. • Clairvoyance is my strongest clair. • I use compassion and empathy. • I am now connecting with my soul.	• Use more clairs. • Delve deeper into the evidence. • Create a stronger connection to the spirit world.	• I am using all my clairs. • I am delving deeper into the evidence. • I am an open channel for the spirit world.	• For the coming year, each morning, close your eyes and meditate for a few minutes on your affirmations. • Visualize yourself as already doing what you hope to accomplish.

EXERCISE 2

Repeat an Exercise

Objective 2:

Reflect on all you've learned as you've worked through this book. Choose an exercise you'd like to repeat, and compare your current video recording of this reading to the first video recording you recorded when you did the exercise.

Instructions for Exercise 2:

1. Choose the exercise.
2. Re-watch the video example of the exercise you want to try again (Optional).
3. Grab any handouts related to the exercise you have chosen.
4. Set your intent.
5. Hit "Record" on your phone or recorder.
6. Do the reading.
7. Stop the recording.

Discussion with Group, Partner (or Yourself) About the Process, Exercise, and Your Growth:

Take a look at the handout with your group or partner. Or, you may want to do this evaluation by yourself. It's your choice.

- Were you able to bring forward evidence the sitter wanted?
- If yes, were you able to go deep within the evidence?
- Were there any pieces of evidence for which the sitter was able to coach you to go deeper?
- If yes, were you able to go deeper?
- Did a story begin to form from your evidence? If yes, which parts were key? If no, what could you have done differently?
- Watch the first video recording of you doing this exercise to compare your first attempt to what you have just done. In which areas do you see growth?
- Which area do you feel needs more work going forward?

Journal:

- Reflect on how you feel about your reading today. Write down your thoughts.
- Share any emotions or struggles that may have come up.
- What did you feel your strengths were? Where did you have challenges? What growth did you see after watching the first video?
- What was your gold nugget, the best bit of the reading?
- Reflect on where you were at the beginning of this book. Where are you now? Where would you like to go next?
- Reflect on your plan going forward. Write down your thoughts.
- Close your eyes, take a few deep breaths, and ask your soul what wisdom it wants to leave with you today. Wait for it to come. Start writing.

—— ୭୭ ——

A mighty wind blew night and day.
It stole the oak tree's leaves away.
Then snapped its boughs and pulled its bark
Until the oak was tired and stark.
But still the oak tree held its ground
While other trees fell all around.
The weary wind gave up and spoke,
"How can you still be standing, Oak?"
The oak tree said, "I know that you
Can break each branch of mine in two,
Carry every leaf away
Shake my limbs, and make me sway.
But I have roots stretched in the earth,
Growing stronger since my birth.
You'll never touch them, for you see,
They are the deepest part of me.
Until today, I wasn't sure
Of just how much I could endure.
But now I've found, with thanks to you,
I'm stronger than I ever knew.

—Johnny Ray Ryder, Jr.

—— ୭୭ ——

Serving Spirit

Professional mediums sacrifice a lot to polish their craft, and the road isn't always easy. Sometimes it is a long and lonely journey. You travel to the depths of your soul, and as you heal on every level, that healing prepares you for the next step. The rewards of your journey—individual growth, personal empowerment, and spiritual advancement—give you access to the spirit world. Those in the spirit world hold you close and are proud of your dedication to serve Spirit.

When you compile a treasure chest of invaluable methods and techniques and stretch your clairs, you establish a strong foundation for your mediumship work. I urge you to continue polishing your craft. The world needs strong, ethical, skilled mediums. Stand true to the sacredness of your work. You are the new innovators. So, be the best you can be, write your own story, create a legacy to inspire the mediums of the future.

As you move forward, enjoy the ride. Celebrate every contact with the spirit world you make as a miracle. Expect the unexpected. Just when you think you have it all figured out, changes occur. Go with the flow. Trust that your spirit team has everything under control, that they are always working for your highest good. Spend more time with your spirit team—they are your partners so include them in all you do spiritually. They are your first teachers and are far wiser than we are here in the physical world.

Continue practicing the exercises in this book. Find your tribe to work alongside you. Below I have listed a few resources to help you as you move forward.

RESOURCES

- Visit my website at *https://www.kayreynolds.org* often for updates on classes, lectures, mentorships, and video support with the exercises.
- Facebook Group Medium's Corner: https://facebook.com/groups/mediumscorner
- Facebook Page: https://www.facebook.com/mediumkayreynolds
- YouTube channel: http://www.youtube.com/c/MediumKayReynolds
- Arthur Findlay College, Stansted, England: https://www.arthurfindlaycollege.org
- Jason Goldsworthy: www.jasongoldsworthy.com
- Paul Jacobs: www.mediumpauljacobs.com
- Mavis Pittilla: www.mavispittilla.com

It is my wish for you that you recognize the spirit within now and recognize the power you have within yourself. Continue to go within, continue to journal with your soul, and continue to build your power. Remember, all you do in this work depends on your soul connection and your power. The stronger these two become, the more polished as a medium you will become. Everything you need is held within you. When in doubt, search your soul. When your mediumship feels rocky, go within. All knowledge, all knowing, and all your tools are within you, waiting to help you. You are a perfect expression of your Creator. Shine your light.

AFTERWORD

I want to leave you with an impromptu writing piece I did before I began writing this book. I was procrastinating getting started, allowing thoughts of self-doubt to control my actions. It was similar to getting started on my spiritual journey. I had chatter in my head. It was saying: "Who am I to think I could write a book? And who am I to think anyone would read it?" As I sat on my porch in the wee hours one morning, admiring the stars barely shining through as the sun crept over the mountain ridge, this piece of writing began to unfold. I hope you enjoy it.

As I woke up this morning, I heard the words "Whatcha waiting on?" That happens to me a lot as I wake from slumber. I may hear words whispered in my ear or a thought runs through my mind. Sometimes I get a feeling of knowing something without knowing how I know it. It's crazy I know. But that's me. It's who I am. I embrace my weirdness. I do.

This day was no different. I opened my eyes. I heard a whisper ask, "Whatcha waiting on?" I thought about it, wondered what it meant, and left it there. It would come to me sooner or later. It always does. Coffee was far more important. I poured my first cup, fed the cats, and stepped outside on the deck to take in the beauty of the Smokey Mountains. It's my favorite place, my deck. I breathe in the energy of the mountains, and the energy of the ancestors as my own ancestors draw near. Sometimes my mom, dad, grandparents, and others come and join me too.

I love when they draw near. I feel their love like never before. It's so pure. So forgiving. And gentle. Oh my, is it ever gentle. I sit and they wrap their love around me. They talk to me. I share my fears and they reassure me that all is as it needs to be, and remind me of the strength I hold within. I share my dreams and in my mind's eye I can see them showing me the key that unlocks the wisdom buried deep within my soul. They don't tell me what to do. I wish they would. That's for sure. But instead they just remind me that I have all the tools within to do whatever I choose. I cherish my time with all of them. I really do.

I gaze at the mountains and wonder if the ancestors can see what I see. I invite them to come closer. I tell them to use my eyes if they wish. I feel them. The usual chatter racing through my mind begins to slow down as they come closer still. The energy they bring is strong. I find myself beginning to move with the energy, swaying side to side for a while. Then it changes, swaying forward, then backward, and my movements change to match theirs.

I breathe. I say a prayer for Mother Earth and all her inhabitants. I ask for healing for those in need and I thank God for another day on Earth. My mind becomes still. Suddenly all that is going on around me becomes muted. The sounds of the birds become distant. Indy, the cat, who is trying oh so hard to get her older brother to play with her as she runs from one end of the deck to the other, begins to fade from my awareness.

My breathing becomes rhythmic, my mind calms, the silence arrives. I am breathing in and out, falling deeper into the silence of my soul.

I breathe again. I'm there—as if I'm transported in time to a place of serenity—high above the valley on a ridge in the Smokey Mountains. I've been here many times before. It feels so familiar. Like home. I gaze off into the distance and just know that what I see is Tennessee. I know, without knowing how I know, that Georgia is to my left and North Carolina is below my feet. I love this place. That's for sure. I feel a connection that runs deep into my soul.

Drifting deeper into my meditation, I become aware of my ancestors joining me on the ridge.

This is their home. They know this ridge, these mountains, and the memories the mountains hold. They reach out to me and I take their hands. Heartache pierces through me. Not my heartache, their heartache. Flashes of life as they knew it tumbles through my mind. It's too much to bear. I want the images to go away. Yet I yearn to know more about their life, their story.

Grandfather, from five or maybe six generations back, smiles and motions for me to sit on the ledge. He sits beside me. Without saying a word, he begins to speak to my soul.

I listen.

I watch.

And somehow, I know what he is telling me. He points to the colors of the sky and explains to me the importance of color in the work I do.

He grabs my hand once again. Energy is moving around us—my energy, his energy—it blends into one. Just like that, my colors blend with his colors. His thoughts become my thoughts. This is it. This is where two worlds meet. Where our worlds come together and he becomes my teacher. As much as I want to talk to him, ask him questions, I know that my role is to be still and let information flow from him to me.

And so, I sit.

I listen.

I take it all in.

Time stands still when I'm in this place. I become lost in the words of my grandfather. I love this space. I feel safe. I feel love. It feels familiar, like I'm home.

Over my shoulder, I can feel the eyes of an ancestor I call Mama. I don't know why I call her Mama. It just falls from my lips when she is around as if it's what I've always called her from many moons ago. Mama is short in stature but mighty in strength. She's endured more than any human should ever have to endure. She tells me she was a medicine woman. I'm not surprised.

She is always showing me plants and when I need healing, Mama comes. My bond with Mama grows by the day. She is as much a part of me as anyone living.

The warmth of her smile draws me to her and I know that my time with them both on this ridge is coming to an end. I don't want to leave but I know I must. My lessons for the day are over.

And just like that, I see the two of them standing on the ridge smiling and waving as I slip away, back to the deck, into the rocking chair, surrounded by the sounds of birds and the cats fighting. Just like that.

I take a deep breath, wiggle my toes, and here I sit. The full cup of coffee I had to have right away is cold. I don't mind. I know now the meaning of the question I heard upon waking. Funny how that happens.

I warm my coffee and somehow find my way to my computer. It wasn't in my morning plans to sit at the computer. Sitting at the computer means only one thing: work. I think, "Really? Do we have to do this now? Can I not have a hot cup of coffee first?"

The computer boots up. The strangest thing happens. There on my screen is a video of a book publisher, laying out the steps of how to get your book published. How did that happen?

I can tell you this. When the spirit world asks you a question upon waking, and then your guides lead you into a deep meditation before you ever get a sip of your much-needed coffee, it might be a good idea to listen. Because if you try not to listen, they will only find another way to get their message to you. That's it. That's all I'm saying on that.

So here I sit at my computer, writing because Lord forbid I should stray from this morning's question: "Whatcha waiting on?"

I'll tell you what I'm waiting on. I'm waiting on me.

I'm waiting on me to find the strength that you tell me I have buried deep within my soul.

I'm waiting on me to unlock the wisdom you say I carry with me from many moons ago. I'm waiting on me. That's what I'm waiting on.

I'm waiting on me to believe in myself. I'm waiting on me to take the first step.

I'm waiting on me to see what others have seen in me for a lifetime. It's me. It's me I'm waiting on.

Just me.

I'm waiting for my soul to rise, for my soul to rise and be what it came here to be. That's what I'm waiting on, for my soul to rise.

And just like that, my soul began to rise.

I broke through the wall I had barricaded myself behind. I kicked fear to the curb. I sent self-doubt on its way. I let go of all that was holding me back. Strength, courage, and wisdom began to peek from around the corner. There they all stood. Happy to see me writing. Happy to watch my soul rise and take its place in this world. I began to type. Words began to flow. And as my soul was rising, a tear trickled down my cheek.

That's what happens, you know, when your soul rises. Tears. Tears of joy. Tears of celebration. Tears of freedom as your soul dances in its true light.

Because you see, once you allow your soul to rise, there's no stopping the possibilities.

There's no stopping the momentum. There's no stopping you.

We all have barriers that stop us from doing what our soul has come to do. It's never easy to face your fears. It's never easy to put yourself out there, not knowing if you will have success. It's not easy.

What I've learned is that we all have a purpose here on Earth. If you stray from your soul's purpose, life can become bumpy or even hard. When you are aligned with your soul's path, things are easier. Things begin to happen. And your soul will dance.

Conquer your fears. Kick self-doubt to the curb. Let go of all that is holding you back.

Believe in yourself. See what others see in you. Embrace your purpose.

Set yourself free.

Allow your soul to rise and fly. Whatcha waiting on?

GLOSSARY

Aura: A subtle field of energy emanating from people, animals, or objects that shows who or what they are, physically, emotionally and spiritually.

Auric Field: Layers of subtle fields of energy emanating from the body that are connected to our chakras.

Discarnate: A person or being without a body; in spirit form.

Incarnate: A person or being embodied in flesh or human form.

Mechanics of Mediumship: Techniques or methods used to help you develop the ability to communicate with the spirit world.

Mediumship: The practice of communication between discarnate beings and incarnate beings.

Psychic: Relates to the soul – denotes the ability to receive information from an incarnate soul through the auric field.

Sitter: A person who sits to receive a reading from a psychic or medium.

BIBLIOGRAPHY

Bassett, Jean. *On the Side of Angels*. Stansted: SNU Publications, 1993.

Giesemann, Suzanne. *Droplets of God – The Life and Philosophy of Mavis Pittilla*. nc: One Mind Books, 2019.

Gomes, Jennifer. *Paul – Man of Spirit – The World of Paul Jacobs*. Whitstable: The Holistic Hand, 2008.

Helen Duncan Official Website. www.helenduncan.org 2019.

Higginson, Gordon. Finding the Spirit Within. Arthur Findlay College: Stansted, United Kingdom. Lecture, 1990.

Pittilla, Mavis. *Mavis – With Spirit*. nc: Fantine Press, 1997.

Naylor, William, ed. *Silver Birch Anthology*. Surrey: The Spiritual Truth Press, 2009.

Robertson, Brian, and Simon James. *Magician to Mystic*. Victoria: Tellwell Talent, 2017.

Made in United States
North Haven, CT
16 September 2022

24211210R00168